clipping and grooming your spaniel and setter

ABOUT THE AUTHORS

For eight years Ben Stone was Director of the New York School of Dog Grooming, the first school of dog grooming in the country. For over ten years prior to opening the school, Mr. Stone and his wife, Pearl, operated dog grooming salons in California and New York, and in 1965, collaborated in writing the best selling *Clipping and Grooming Your Poodle* (Arco). In 1967 Ben Stone collaborated with Mario Migliorini in writing *Clipping and Grooming Your Terrier* (Arco), which won an award from the Dog Writers Association. *Clipping and Grooming Your Spaniel and Setter* is the third book by Mr. Stone in the series on dog grooming in the past five years. He has also contributed numerous articles for dog trade publications and is considered an authority in the field of dog grooming.

Mario Migliorini is a former AKC-licenced professional handler of all breeds and has been involved with grooming show dogs for some twenty years. He has handled dogs extensively throughout the United States, and his articles on varied aspects of dog care and training have been published regularly since 1958. Mr. Migliorini and his wife, Margaret, have been involved in breeding, rearing, and conditioning many fine dogs, including their own champion Cockers and English Springers. Mr. Migliorini is a resident of Wyoming, Delaware, where he operates a small exclusive kennel, and is consultant to the New York School of Dog Grooming.

clipping and grooming your spaniel and setter

by ben stone & mario migliorini

ARCO PUBLISHING COMPANY, INC.
New York

Published by ARCO PUBLISHING COMPANY, INC.
219 Park Avenue South, New York, N.Y. 10003

Library of Congress Catalog Number: 78-125941

ISBN 0-668-02371-6

Printed in the United States of America

CONTENTS

FOREWORD

We have written this book on the clipping and grooming of the Spaniels and Setters for the same basic reason that we wrote our books on the clipping and grooming of Poodles and Terriers—that is, the almost complete lack of literature existing on the subject, especially as it pertains to pet grooming. Also, we believe we have made an original contribution in the area of photography and illustration.

In addition to the American Cocker, which comes in three varieties—Black, ASCOB, and Parti-color—there are several other members of the Sporting Dog Group which require periodic trimming. These include the English Cocker, English Springer, and the English, Irish, and Gordon Setters. The other Spaniels—Brittany, Clumber, Field, Sussex, and the American Water Spaniel, as well as the Welsh Springer—require only minimal trimming. Of all these breeds, the American Cocker is by far the most popular, and therefore we have used this dog as our main model.

Since the great majority of Cocker owners consider their dogs pets and grooming Cockers for show is the fancy of a small minority, we have proportioned our step-by-step instruction in this book accordingly.

Mario and the English Springer Ch. Sali Lyn's Makers Mark

With the exception of the American Cocker, the balance of the Sporting breeds may all be groomed *basically* the same way. For the sake of proper organization and clarification, therefore, the book is divided into three parts: American Cocker, Grooming For Show, and The Other Sporting Breeds.

In accordance with the old adage that a picture is worth a thousand words, photographer Fred Honig made free use of his talents. He spent innumerable hours shooting for the right angles in order to achieve the maximum sharpness and clarity of the grooming techniques demonstrated by Mario Migliorini.

Finally, we suggest to those who feel they may have an aptitude or special flair for dog grooming, and think of grooming professionally or opening a dog grooming salon, to take the Advanced Course at the New York School of Dog Grooming or the School's Correspondence Course.

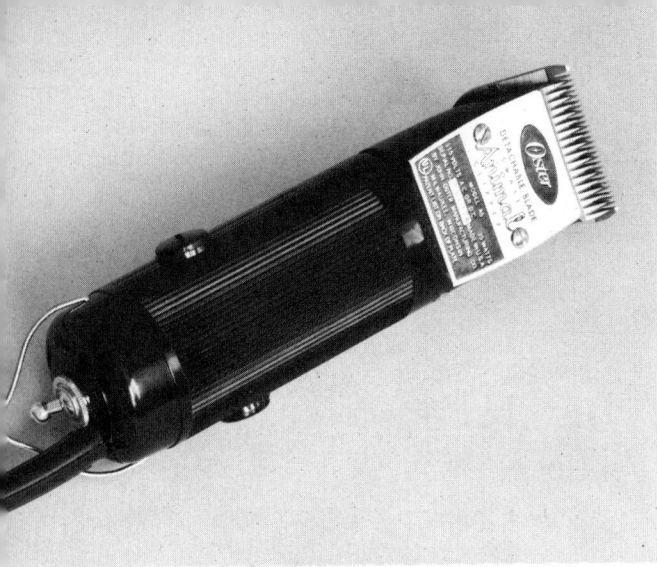

ESSENTIALS OF GROOMING EQUIPMENT

TOOLS OF THE TRADE

OSTER A-5 SMALL ANIMAL CLIPPER—
We recommend this clipper as the best in the world, for either novice or professional. A full range of blades made for this clipper can be snapped on in seconds. There is no need for screwdrivers or extra heads as with other clippers.

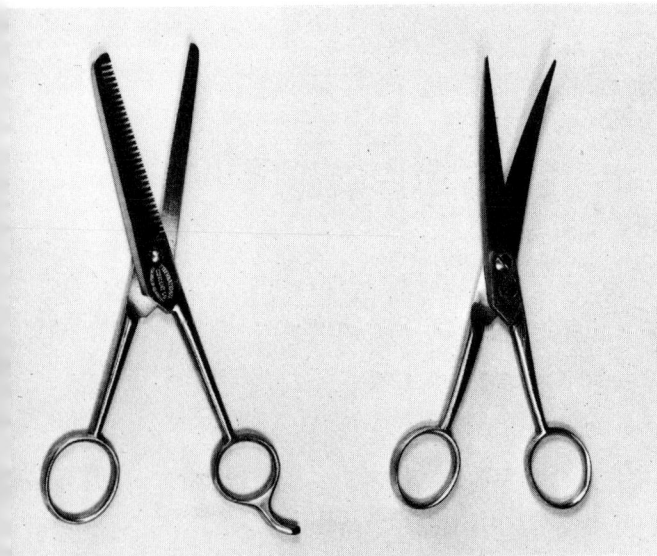

SCISSORS—BARBER & THINNING SHEARS — German-made shears are regarded as the best by the beauty and barber trade; likewise in dog groming. To do a competent job, the terrier groomer should own a pair of good German scissors and thinning shears.

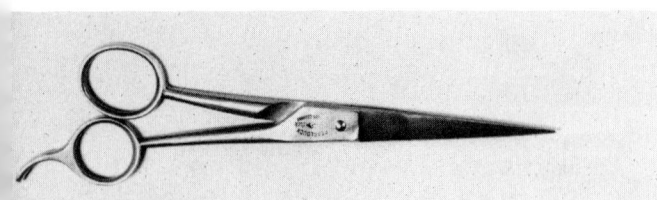

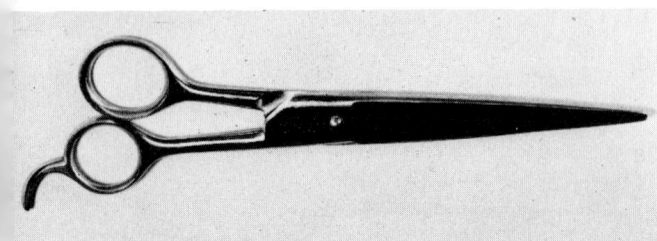

BRUSH—The "Warner" wire slicker is best for all around brushing out the coat. The wire teeth should be neither too harsh nor too soft and they should be set into a foam backing.

COMB—The best all-around comb we can recommend is one with half medium and half fine teeth. The medium side is used first to help tease out mats and tangles or to test for same. The fine side is used for final combing of the coat.

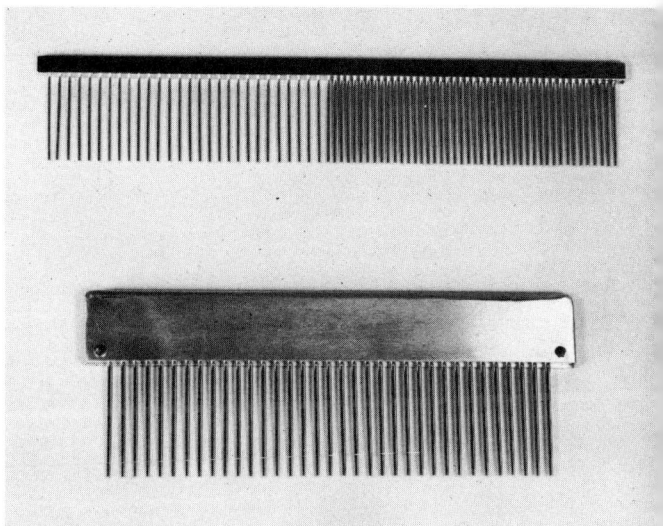

MATTING COMB—A heavy, coarse comb is best for a badly matted coat or for a coat in which foreign matter has become embedded.

NAIL CLIPPERS—The guillotine type of nail clipper illustrated here is the type to which dogs seem to object the least.

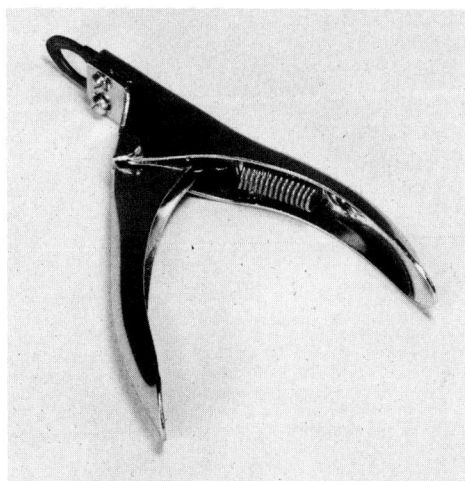

EAR PLUCKERS or HEMOSTATS — The "Kelly" Hemostats are best. This is the straight type which doesn't obstruct the vision and does a good job of plucking the excess hair from the ears.

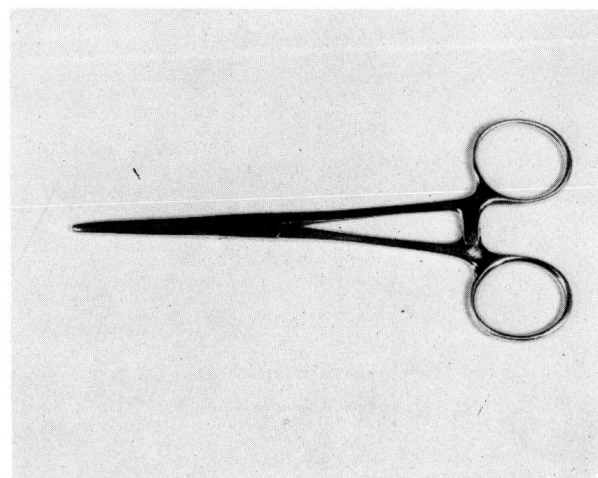

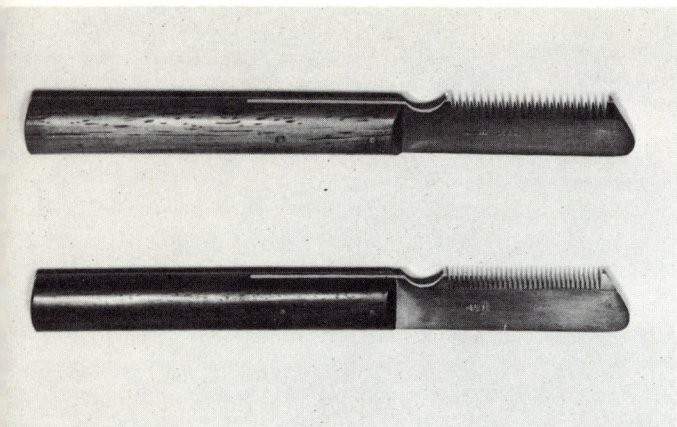

STRIPPING KNIVES—MEDIUM & FINE
—The coarse stripping knife is used for most of the areas to be stripped with the exception of the head and ears, more sensitive areas where the fine stripping knife should be used.

OSTER AIRJET HOME DRYER—This home dryer is adequate for the pet owner who just grooms his own dog. If purchased with hood, it may also be used in milady's boudoir for drying her own hair.

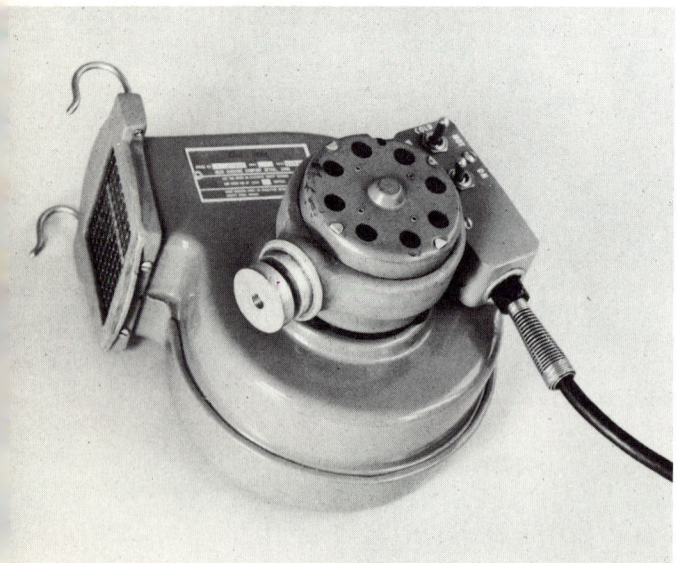

CAGE DRYER—This is a professional dryer especially constructed to be fitted on cages for drying purposes. It has a powerful air flow and dries the average dog in a matter of minutes.

FLOOR DRYER—This type is used mainly for "fluff drying," i.e., drying a damp dog and brushing at the same time where the air flow is being directed at the coat.

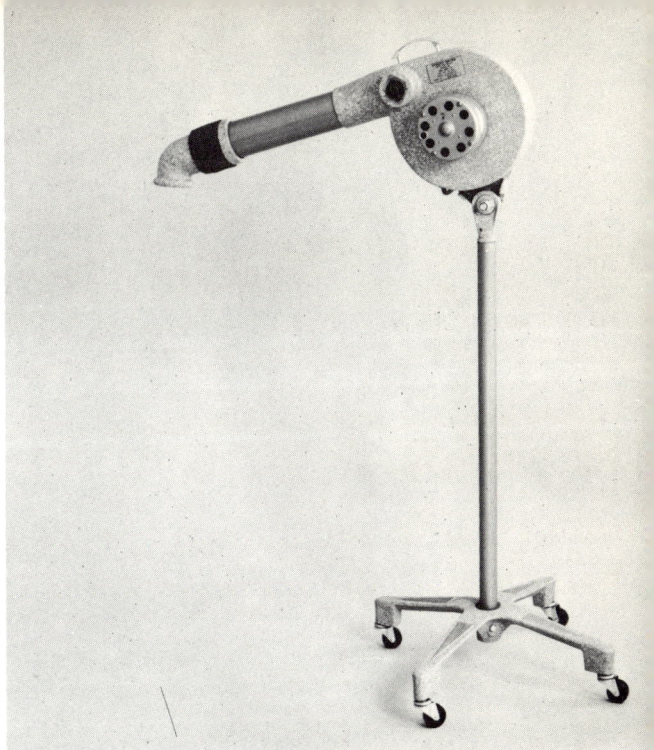

GROOMING TABLE—The traditional grooming table, usually a folding table and easily transported, is 30 inches high; the table measures 24″ x 36″. The ribbed rubber matting on top should be firmly cemented.

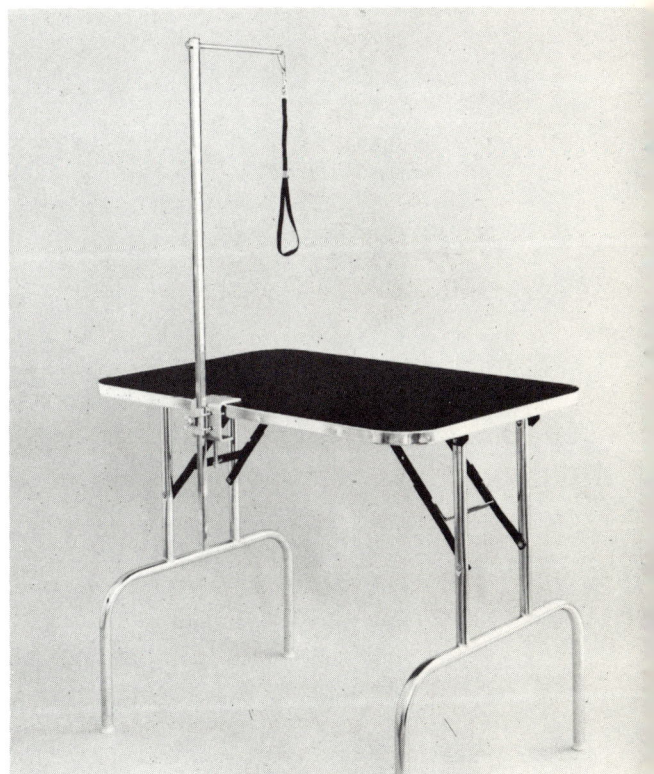

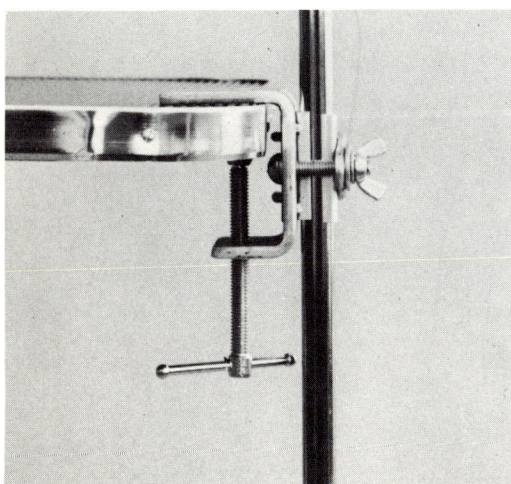

GROOMING POST AND LOOP—The best grooming posts are portable and can be attached to any table. The loop is placed lightly around the dog's neck to prevent the dog from moving or jumping.

Before

After

12

PART I

The American Cocker— Pet Grooming

CHAPTER 1

BRUSHING AND COMBING

The first and most important step in grooming Cockers, in common with all coated breeds, is thorough brushing and combing. The coat must be free of all mats and tangles before being bathed. Otherwise it may become more snarled and even more difficult to comb out.

If your dog is brushed and combed regularly several times each week, this step should only take a few minutes. However, if the dog has not been groomed for a while, time and patience will be required to do a good job. A good coat conditioner applied liberally on a matted coat before brushing will save you wear and tear.

In brushing and combing it is best to start with the dog's hindquarters. This prevents the dog from seeing what is being done and thus gives him less reason to object. In addition, he becomes more easily accustomed to the grooming process. As a safeguard, place a rubber mat under the dog to keep him from slipping or sliding. When brushing, hold part of the dog's coat with one hand to relieve tension.

Start brushing with a light downward motion, keeping the wrist firm but flexible. Grasp the coat firmly with your free hand close to the area that you are brushing to counteract the pull of the brush and to minimize the discomfort to the dog. Use your fingers to part any knots and snarls that do not separate by brushing. The most systematic order of brushing is the following:

1) Legs (*Photos 1-1 and 1-2*). 2) Tail and Head—be especially particular about the ears, fan the fringe over the shoulder (*Photo 1-3*). To brush the opposite side, simply turn the ear over (*Photo 1-4*).

After you are finished with the brushing, use a wide-toothed comb to comb out the feathering. Be just as systematic and methodical with the comb as you were with the brush (*see Photos 1-5, 1-6, and 1-7*).

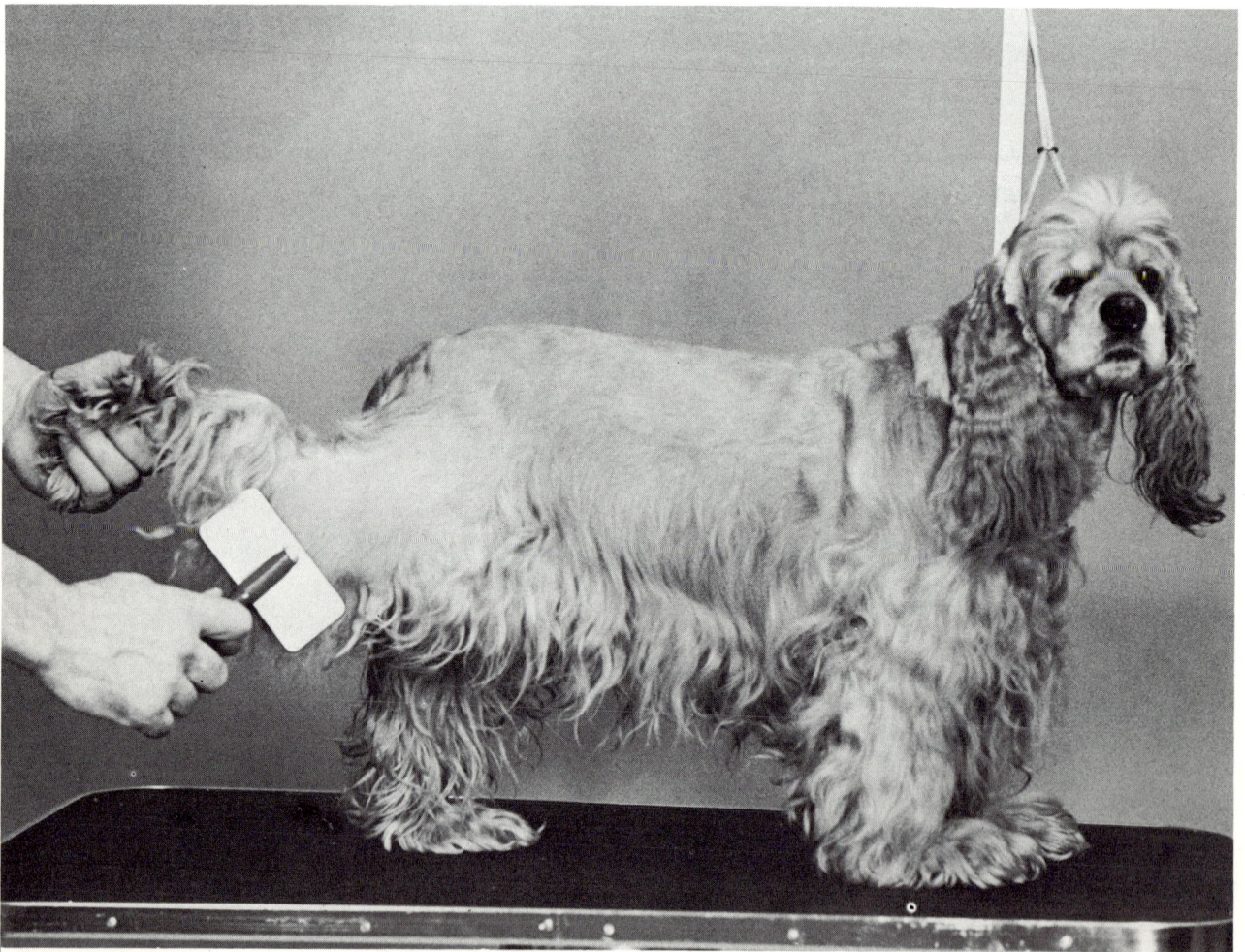

1-1. Brushing Rear Leg

1-2. Brushing Front Leg

1-3. Ear Fringe Over Shoulder

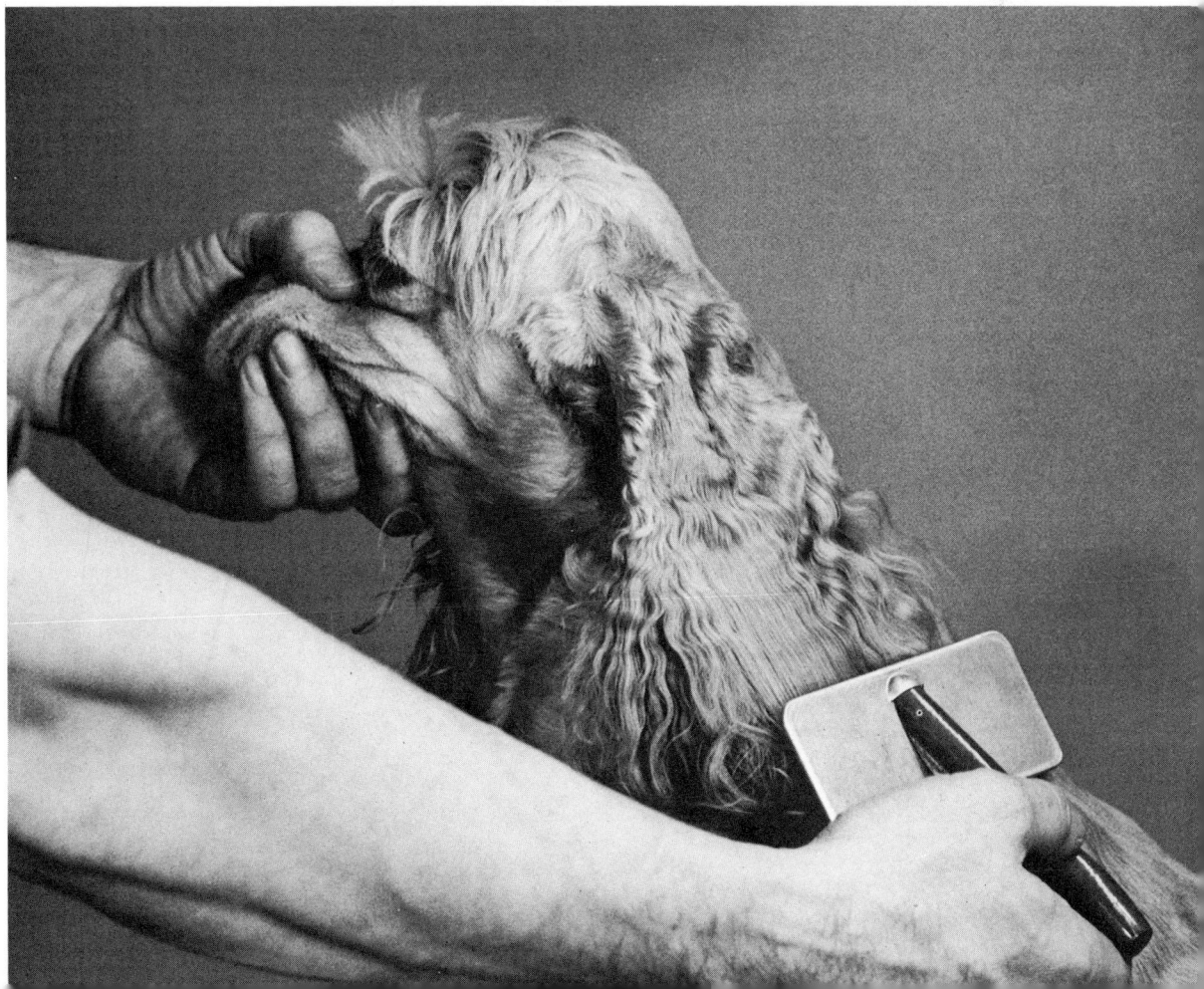

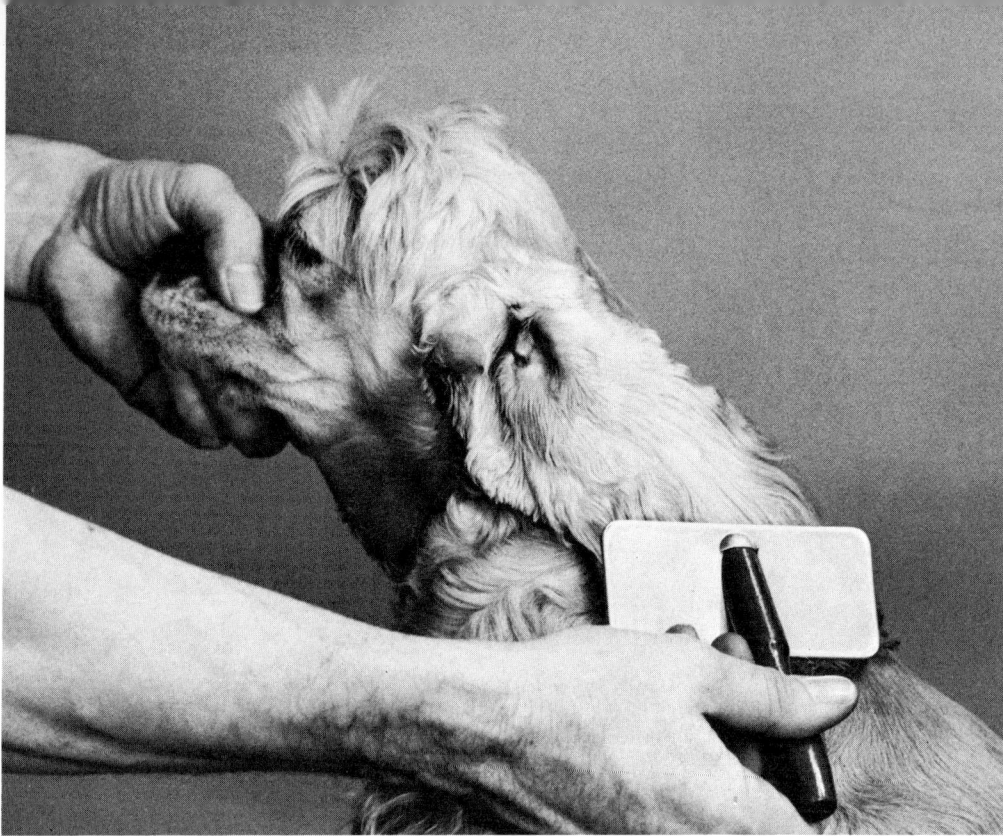

1-4. Turn Ear Over

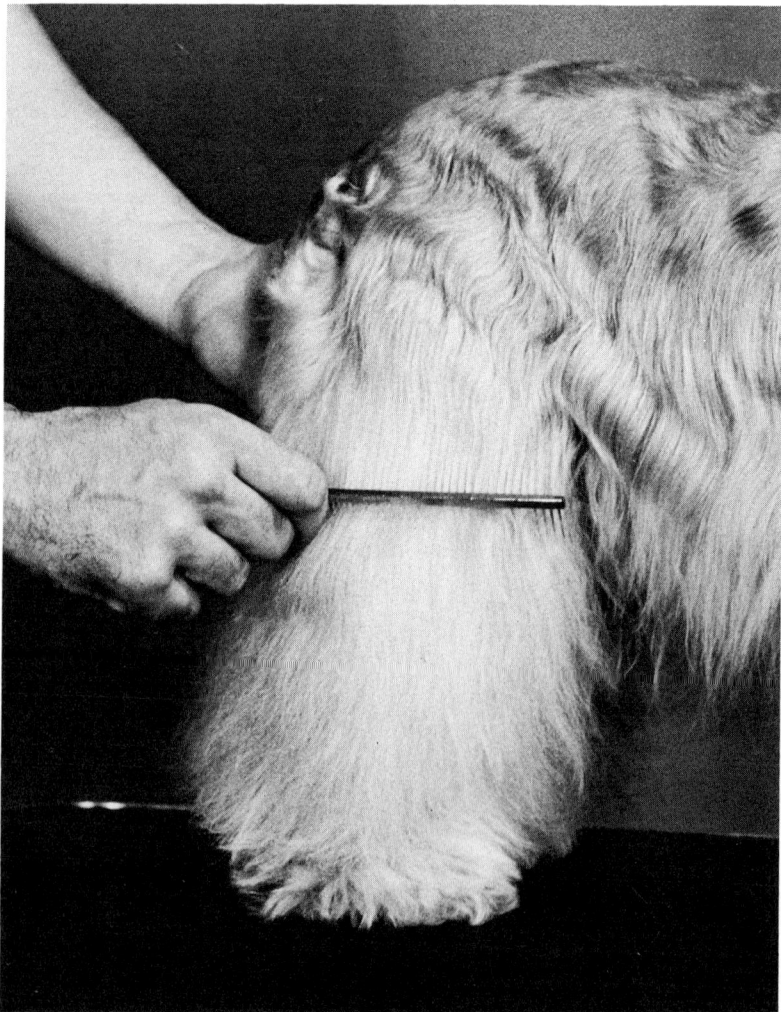

1-5. Combing Rear Leg

The most effective tool yet devised for use on a matted or tangled coat is the "Speedcomb," especially designed for this purpose by co-author Mario Migliorini. To use the "Speedcomb," insert the teeth vertically into the matted area at the outer edge of the coat and lever horizontally with a twisting wrist motion (*Photo 8*). Do not attempt to tear through the mats from the skin level, but work your way toward the skin from the outside. It is recommended that the comb be used cautiously for a while until you get the "hang" of it. When you do, you will find the "Speedcomb" can reduce the time required to comb out any matted coat as much as 50%.

Never underestimate the importance of a thorough brushing and combing. It is the foundation of good grooming. All steps in dog grooming are important, but the most important are brushing and combing.

1-6.   Combing Feathering

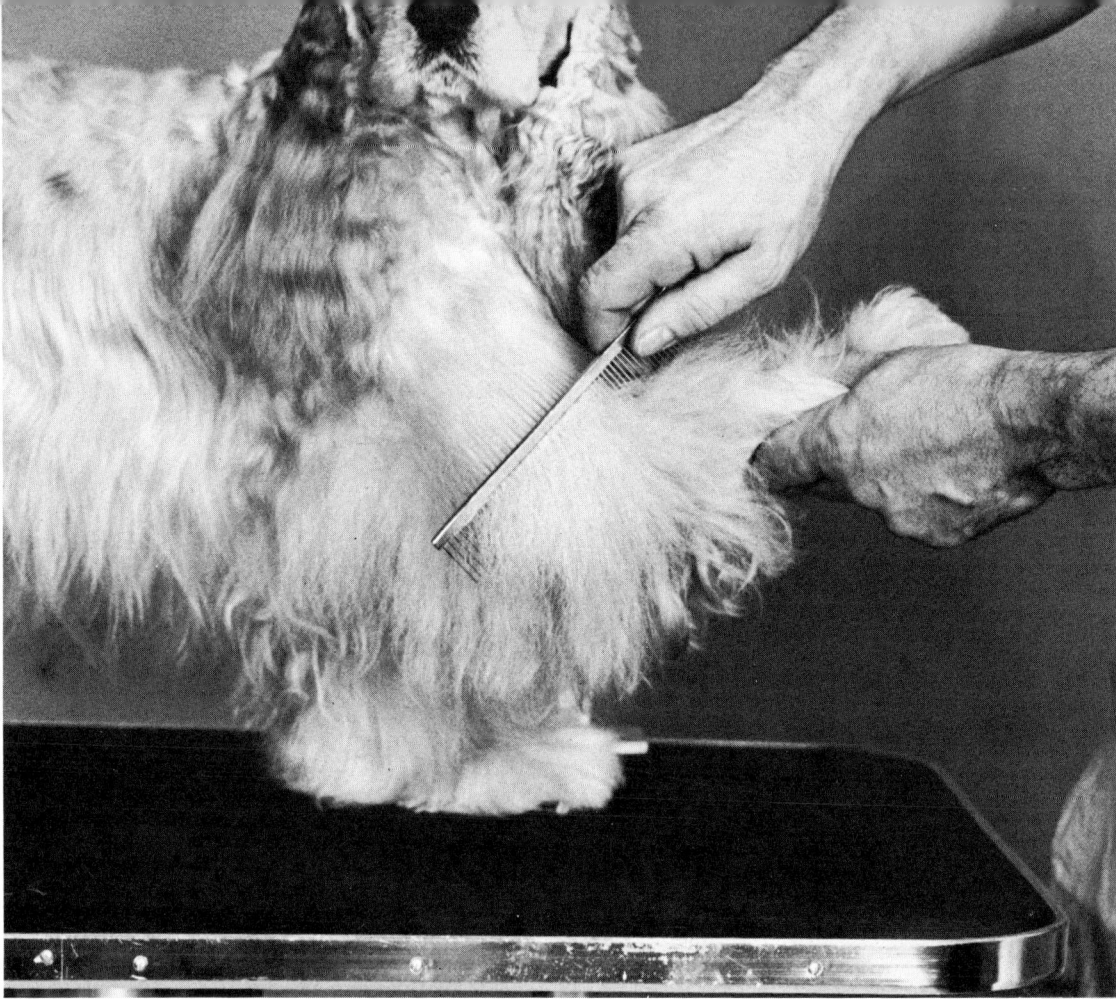

1-7. Combing Front Leg

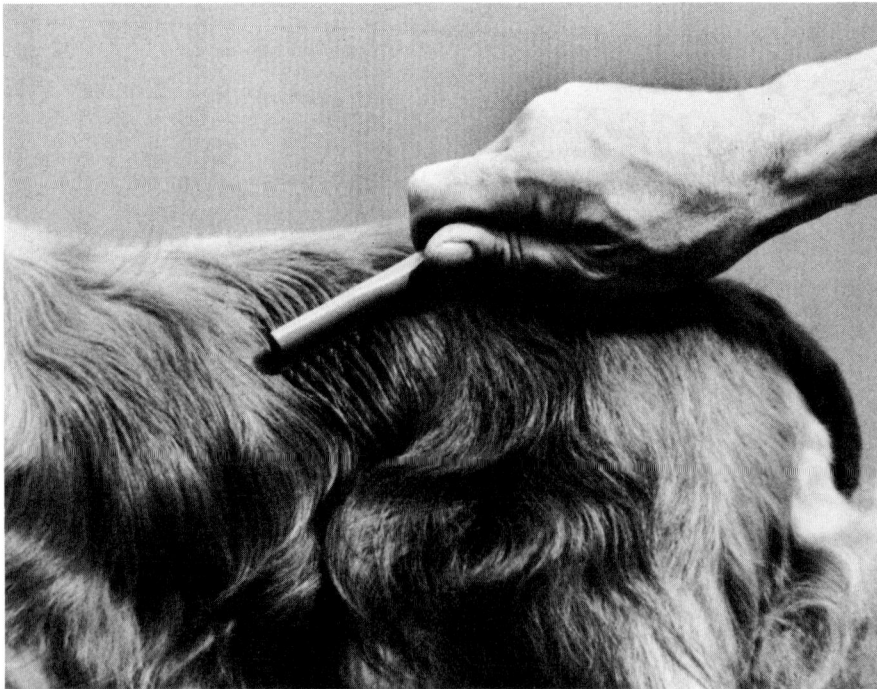

1-8. Speedcomb

CHAPTER 2

BATHING

Keep your Cocker or other sporting dog clean and free of odor, bathing him frequently. We recommend that you bathe the dog at the time of his regular grooming since it is an essential part of the grooming process.

Prepare your materials before putting the dog in the tub. You will need a shampoo, a bristle brush, a sponge, and a towel (*Photo 2-1*). Have everything ready *before* you begin. It's a good idea to wear a plastic apron, since the dog will most likely shake the excess water from his coat and give you a bath, too. If you use a concentrated shampoo, dilute it in a dish first and then saturate the sponge with it. Attach a hose, preferably a shower spray (such as the one shown in the bathing photos) to the faucet to facilitate soaking and rinsing

2-1. Bathtub Materials

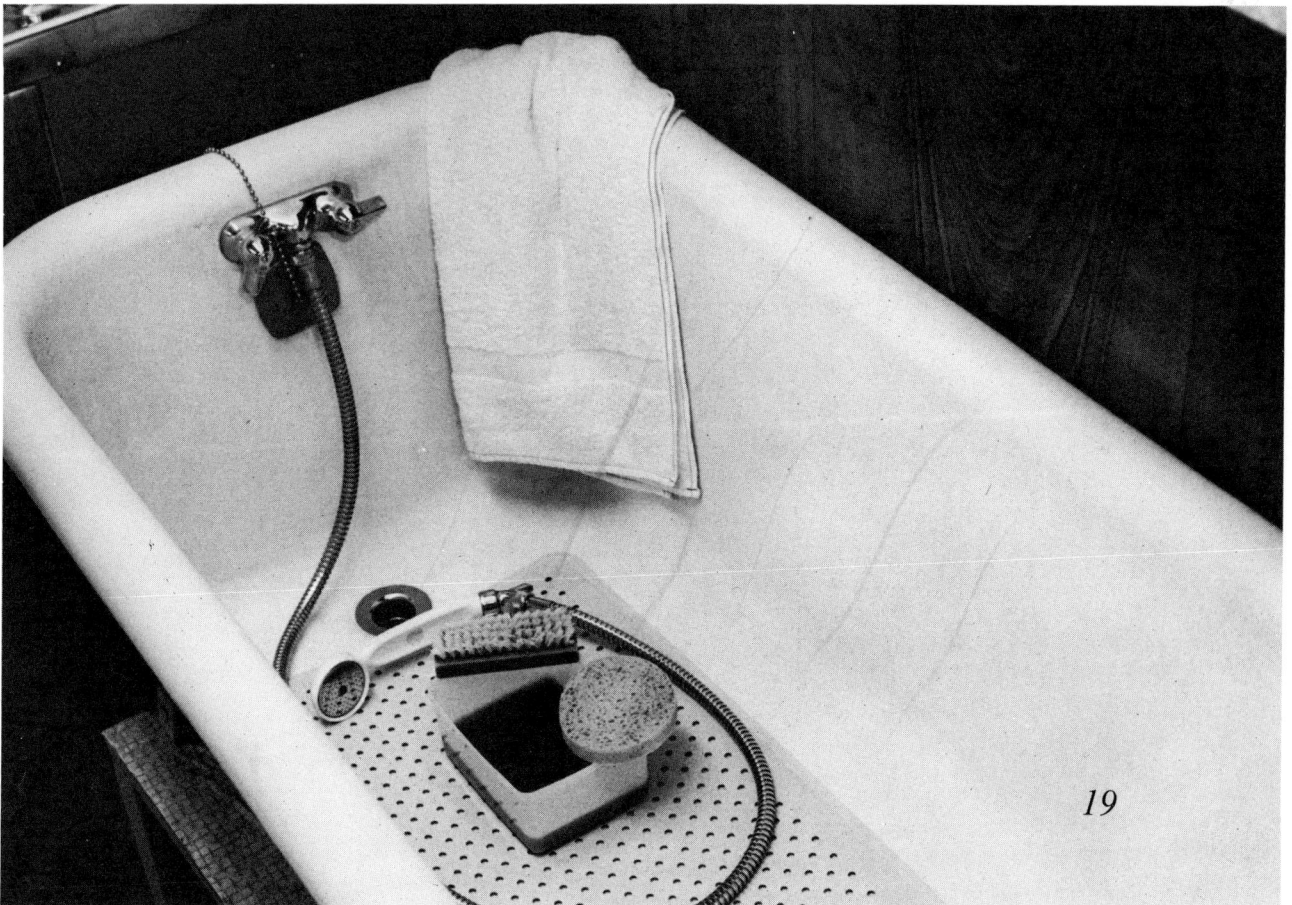

19

the dog. The water should be warm (but not hot), and should always run free, *never* filling the tub.

Soak the dog thoroughly, starting at the rear and working forward (*Photo 2-2*). Pay particular attention to the rectum. Most coats are somewhat water-resistant, so you will have to force the water with your hand through the hair to his skin while you are soaking him. Be careful of his eyes and hold your thumb against the ear canal when you are washing around the dog's ears. Do not put cotton in his ears because water may seep down the canal, placing the thumb against the ear canal will be sufficient to keep water out.

When the dog has been completely soaked, take the shampoo-saturated sponge and begin working up a good lather. Once again, you should move from back to front and pay special attention to the rectum and the pads (the bottom of the paws). These areas are the ones most commonly neglected. Don't be stingy with the soap (*Photo 2-3*).

When you are washing the dog's head, take special care not to get soap in his eyes. A dog will never have the proper attitude toward his bath if it becomes a torturous experience, complete with burning eyes. Use your hands, rather than the sponge, in this area. Novices might even prefer a "no tear" baby shampoo.

The next step is to take a small bristle brush and, using a light rearward motion (*Photo 2-4*), brush the lather into the hair on all parts of the body. Then rinse the dog off from front to rear, being again especially careful of

2-2.   Soaking the Dog

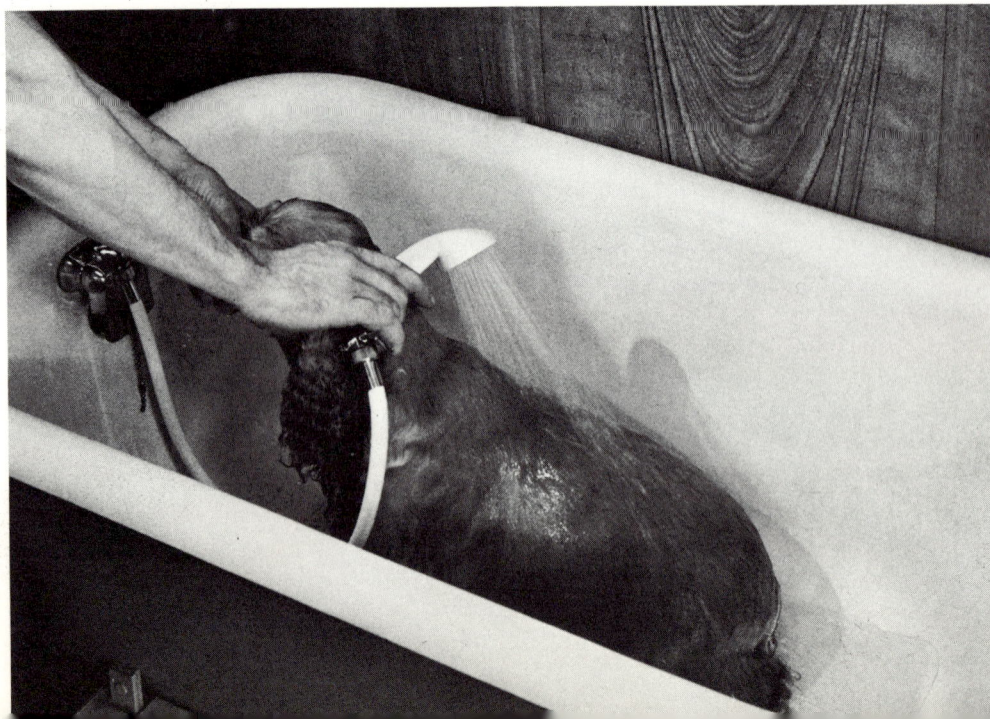

the eyes and ears. Continue rinsing until *all* traces of soap have been washed away (*Photo 2-5*). Any soap remaining in the coat will cause dry skin, itching and flaking.

Gently squeeze the hair on the legs, tail, ears, and all parts of the dog's body with your hands to remove excess water; then rub him briskly with the towel (*Photo 2-6*). Place the dog under a dryer and dry thoroughly before you brush and comb once again.

To keep the dog clean between groomings, simply wipe over his entire coat with a cloth dipped in a dry shampoo and towel dry.

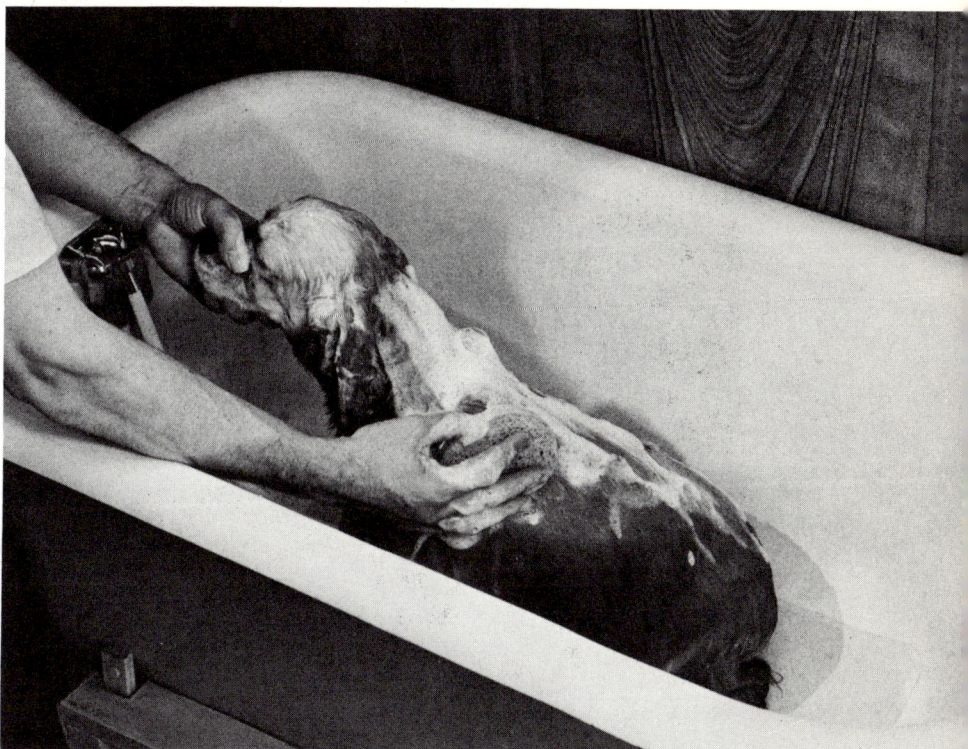

2-3. Sponging Soap

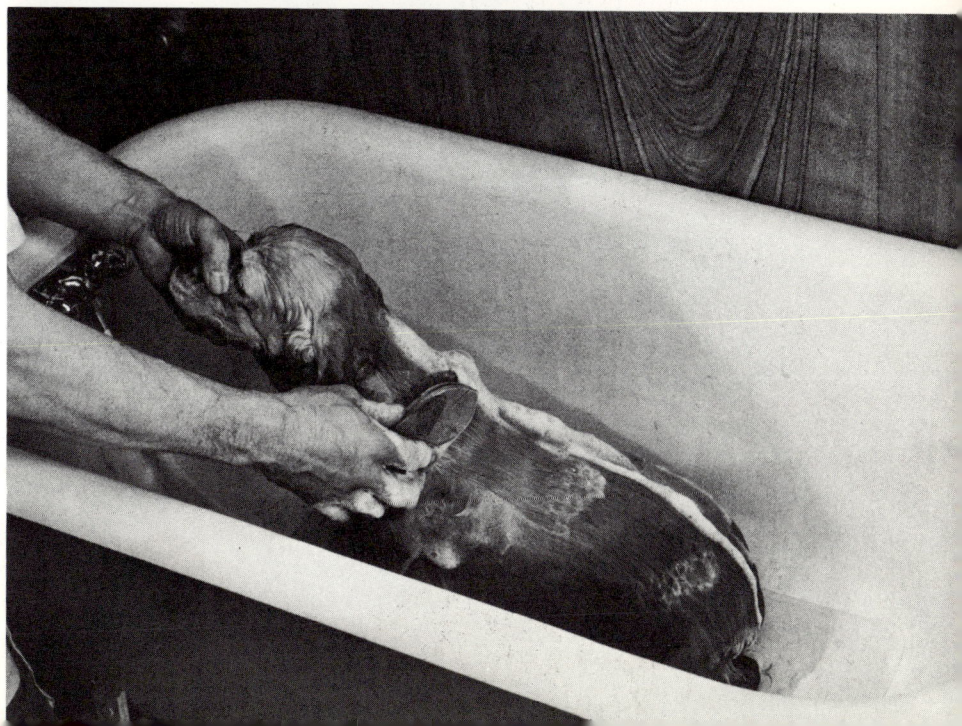

2-4. Brushing in Soap

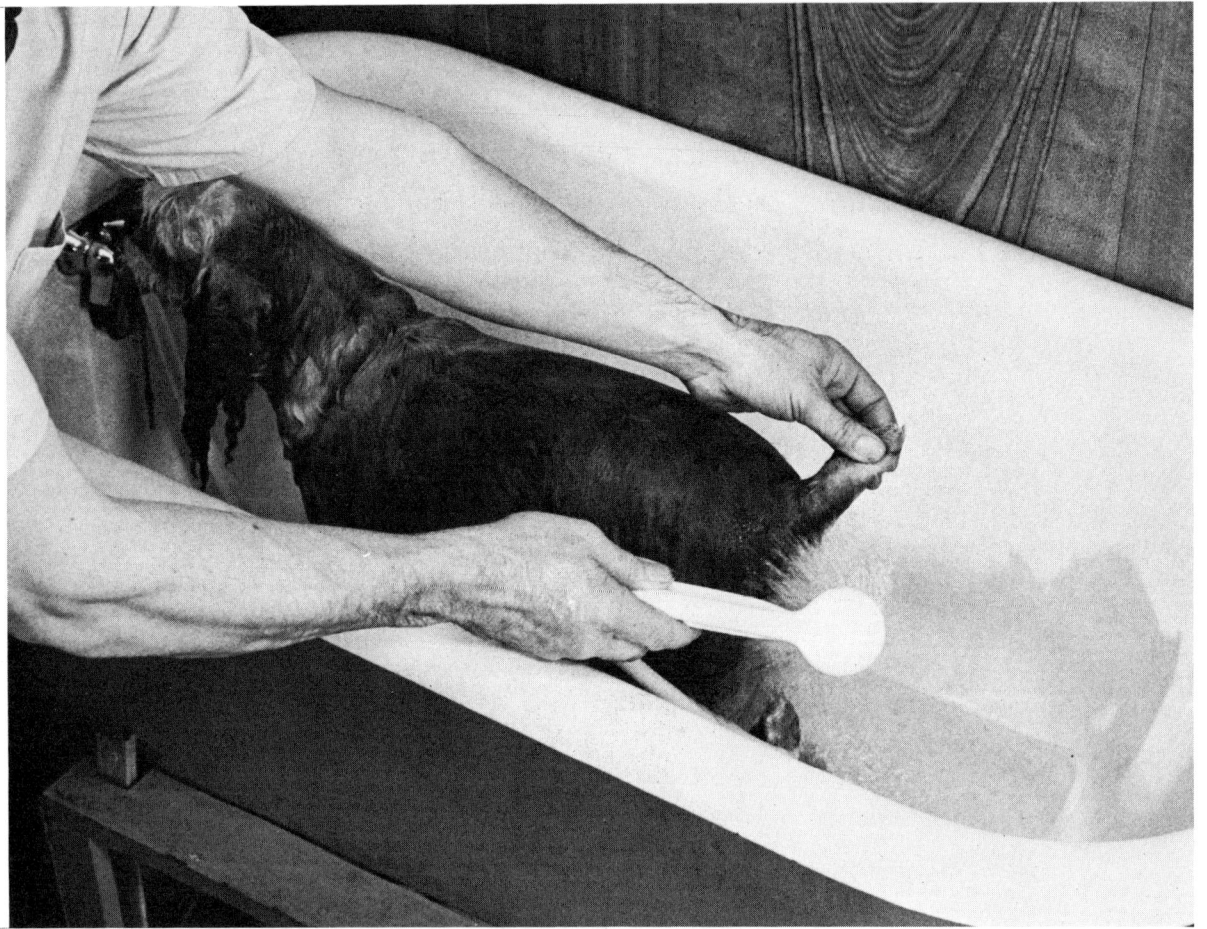

2-5. Rinsing

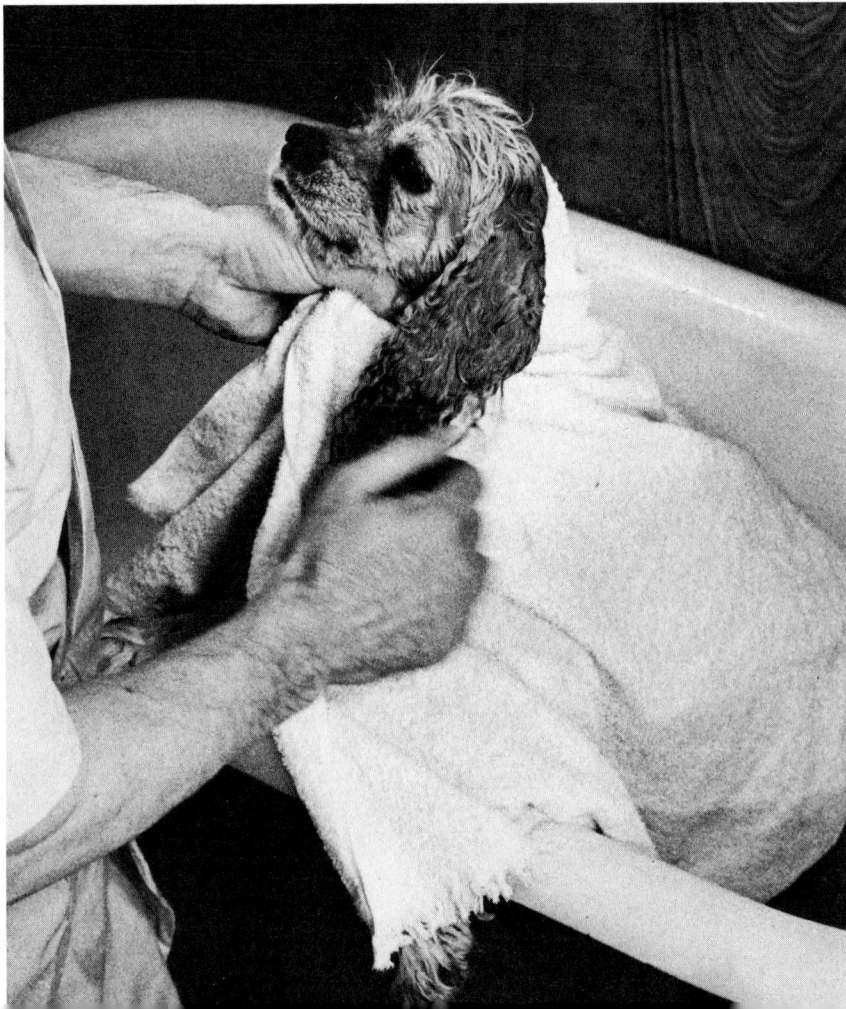

2-6. Toweling

CHAPTER 3

HANDLING AND CONTROL

Lack of control can lead to some very awkward positions while you are grooming your dog. The motto of our school is "Firmness plus Gentleness." Although an obedient dog is a prerequisite to good grooming, the entire procedure requires the handler to be both firm and gentle. Firmness does not mean roughness or brutality, but the dog must know who is the master and that his grooming period is not a time for play or petting.

Think in terms of training a child. With a youngster we can be both firm in our demands and gentle in our manner of enforcing them. Of course, the owner of a spoiled dog has one advantage over the parents of a spoiled child —the dog in need of special correction can be referred to a dog obedience trainer.

The question of handling and control, or the proper combination of firmness and gentleness, is not as simple as it might seem, especially for the novice who is making his first attempts at grooming a dog. The tendency is to let the dog have his own way. But the novice will soon learn that grooming then can become an ordeal rather than a pleasant experience

What is the right combination of firmness and gentleness? There can be no precise answer, and we can only say that experience may be the best teacher.

A dog should become accustomed to being groomed while he is still a puppy. Then he will not present a problem when he grows up. In those exceptional cases where the dog has become extremely spoiled and unmanageable or has been mistreated, it may be difficult to do a good grooming job.

Controlling Your Dog on the Table

When the dog is on the grooming table (there should always be a rubber mat on the table top) you can control him by holding him lightly with your hand between his rear legs. If the dog moves or attempts to sit down, gentle

23

pressure will bring him back into the right position. Don't re-position the dog by lifting him under the stomach, because he will roach up.

You cannot achieve maximum control unless both you and the dog are comfortable. If either of you is uncomfortable during the grooming process, the dog is not being handled properly. A good deal of common sense must enter into this relationship. For example, during each stage of the grooming there are logical times for either the dog or you to sit down. But the dog must also stand when standing is required and stay when so commanded.

The use of the grooming post and loop is frequently necessary and can be a great aid to better handling and control (*See Photo 1-1, Chapter 1*).

CHAPTER 4

CLIPPING

Body Pattern

Study the anatomy of the Cocker so you will gain some familiarity with the nomenclature (*Diagram 1*).

We will start our clipping by doing the body first since this is easiest for the beginner. A No. 10 or No. 7 blade can be used on the body. The No. 10 gives a closely clipped look, the No. 7 a more natural appearance. In the demonstration we are using a No. 7 for the body pattern. Using the spine as a guideline, clip down the back of the neck from the base of the skull to the withers (*Photo 4-1*) and from the withers to the base of the tail (*Photo 4-2*). Then clip down the side of the neck to a point of the shoulder approximately midway between the withers and the elbow (*Photo 4-3*). Continue clipping over the side of the body with sweeping strokes following the contour of the dog (*Photo 4-4*). Work in the direction of the lay of the coat, from front to back along a line extending from the point of the sternum to the point of the rump (*Photo 4-5*). Use slightly overlapping strokes. *Do not* clip legs and skirt (*see Diagram 2*).

Tail

Using the same blade as on the body, clip from the base to the tip of the tail on all sides. Try to achieve a round, slightly tapered effect (*Diagram 3*). The area under the tail should be clipped close (*Photo 4-6*).

Stomach

Using a No. 10 blade, clip the stomach area to the navel. Trim the excess hair around the penis of male dogs. To facilitate clipping the stomach, grasp the dog by the front legs, above the elbows, and raise the dog up so that it is standing on its hind legs (*Photo 4-7*).

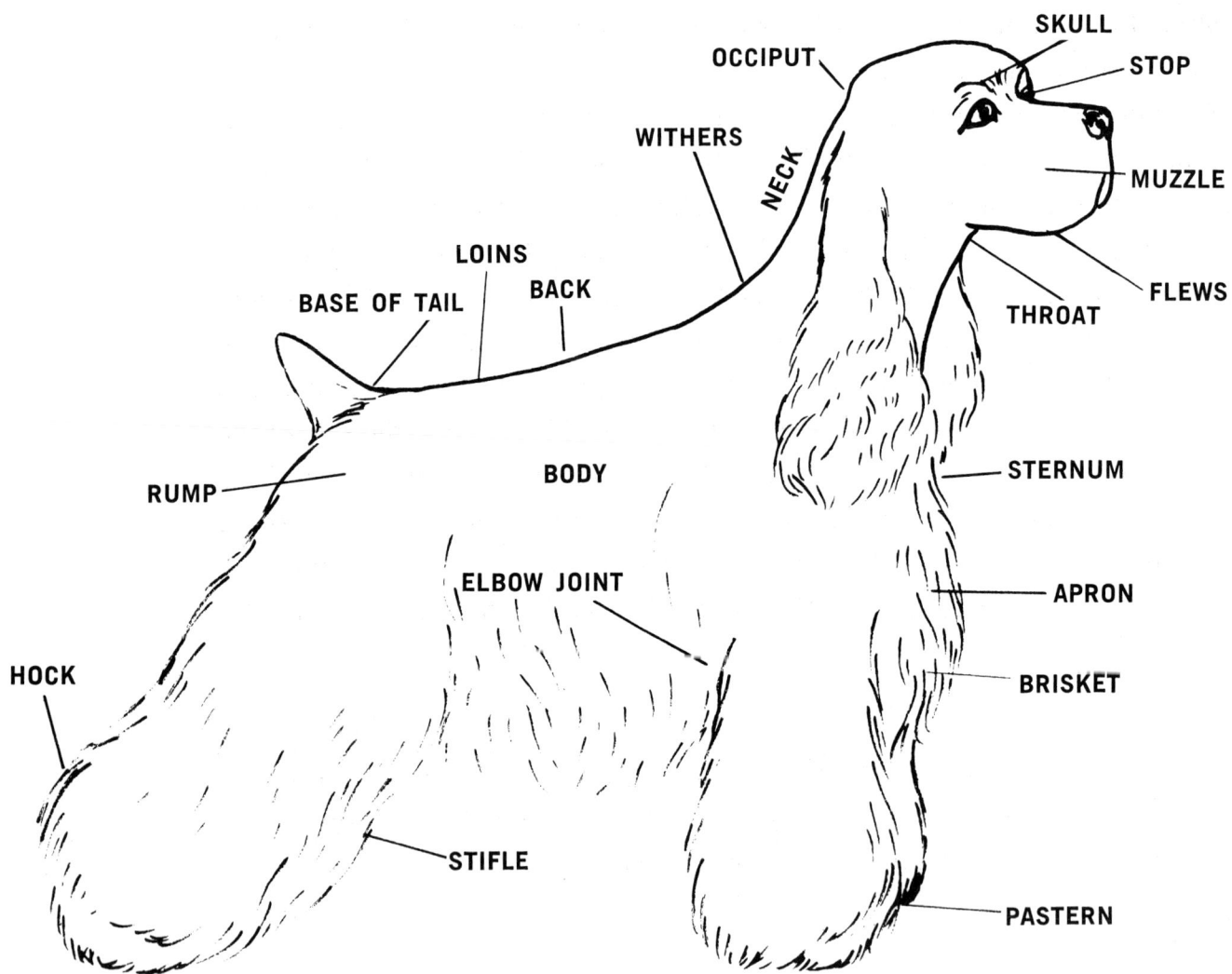

SKULL

OCCIPUT

STOP

WITHERS

NECK

MUZZLE

LOINS

FLEWS

BASE OF TAIL

BACK

THROAT

RUMP

BODY

STERNUM

ELBOW JOINT

APRON

BRISKET

HOCK

STIFLE

PASTERN

Diagram 1. American Cocker—Anatomy

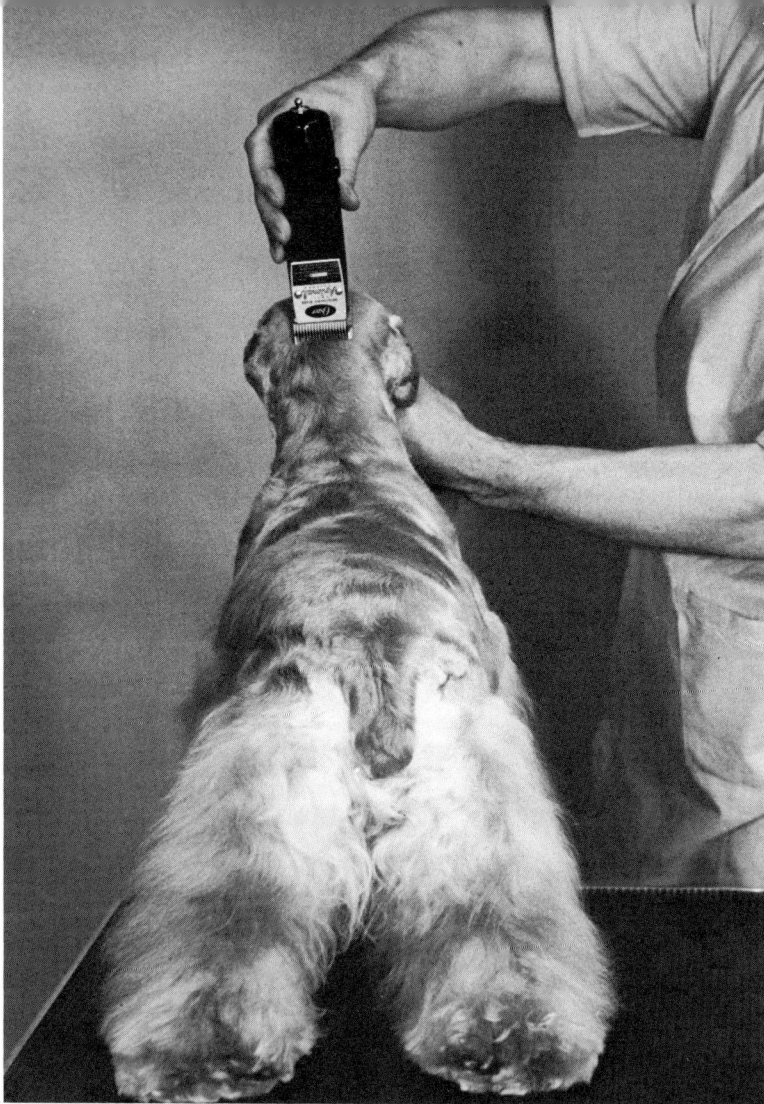

4-1. Clipping from Skull to Withers

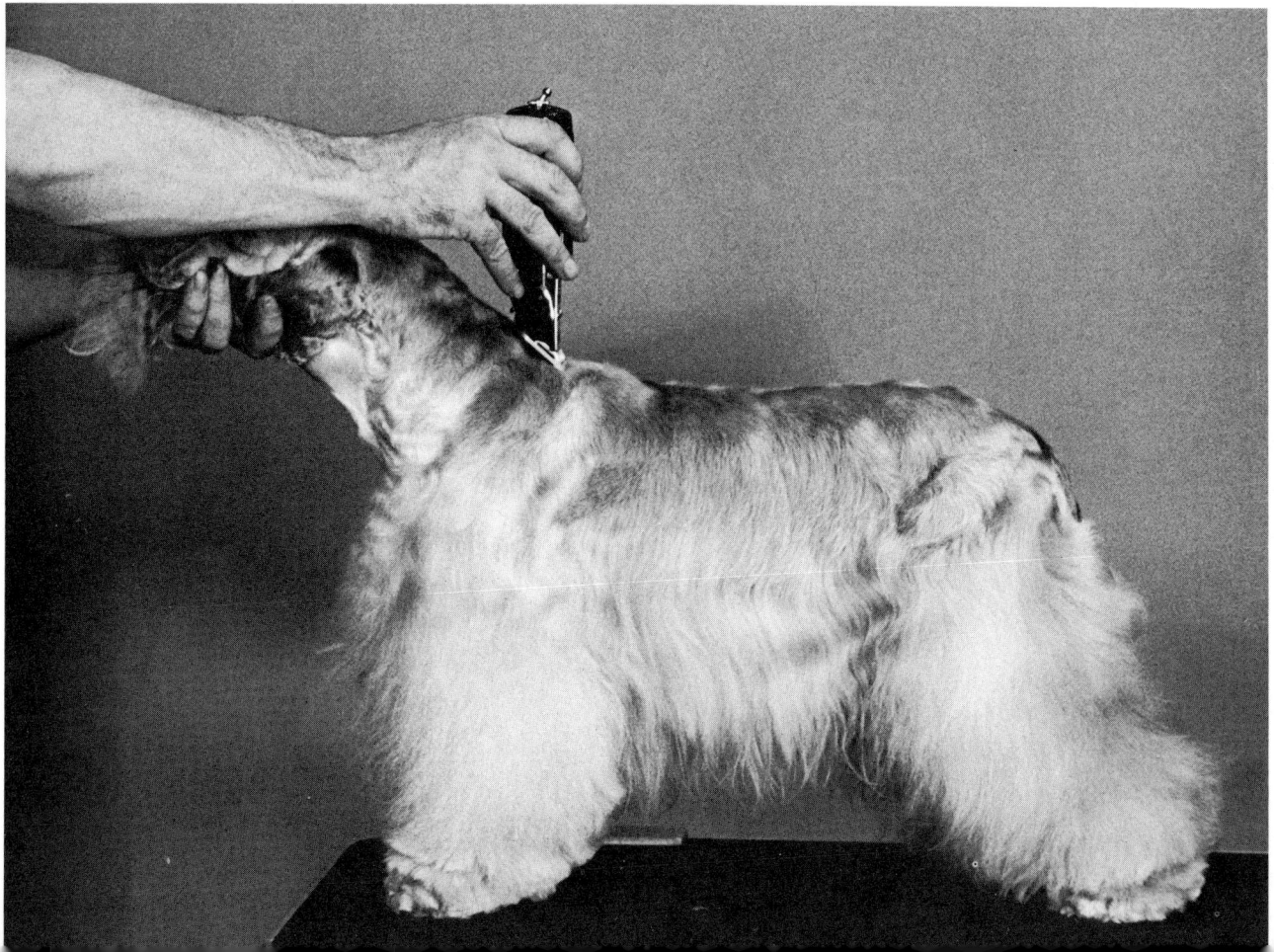

4-2. Clipping from Withers to Tail

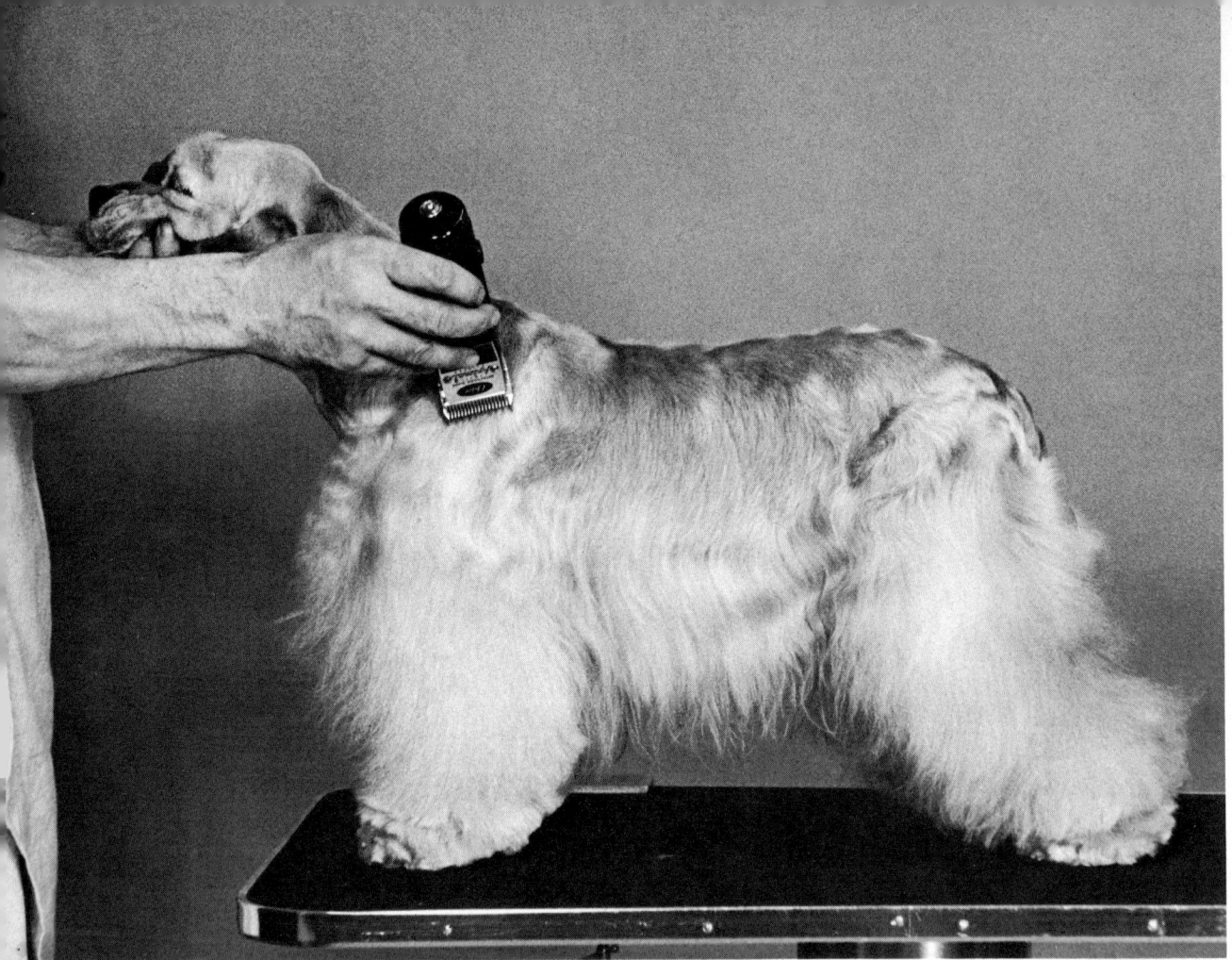

4-3.   Clipping from Withers to Elbow

4-4.   Clipping with Contour

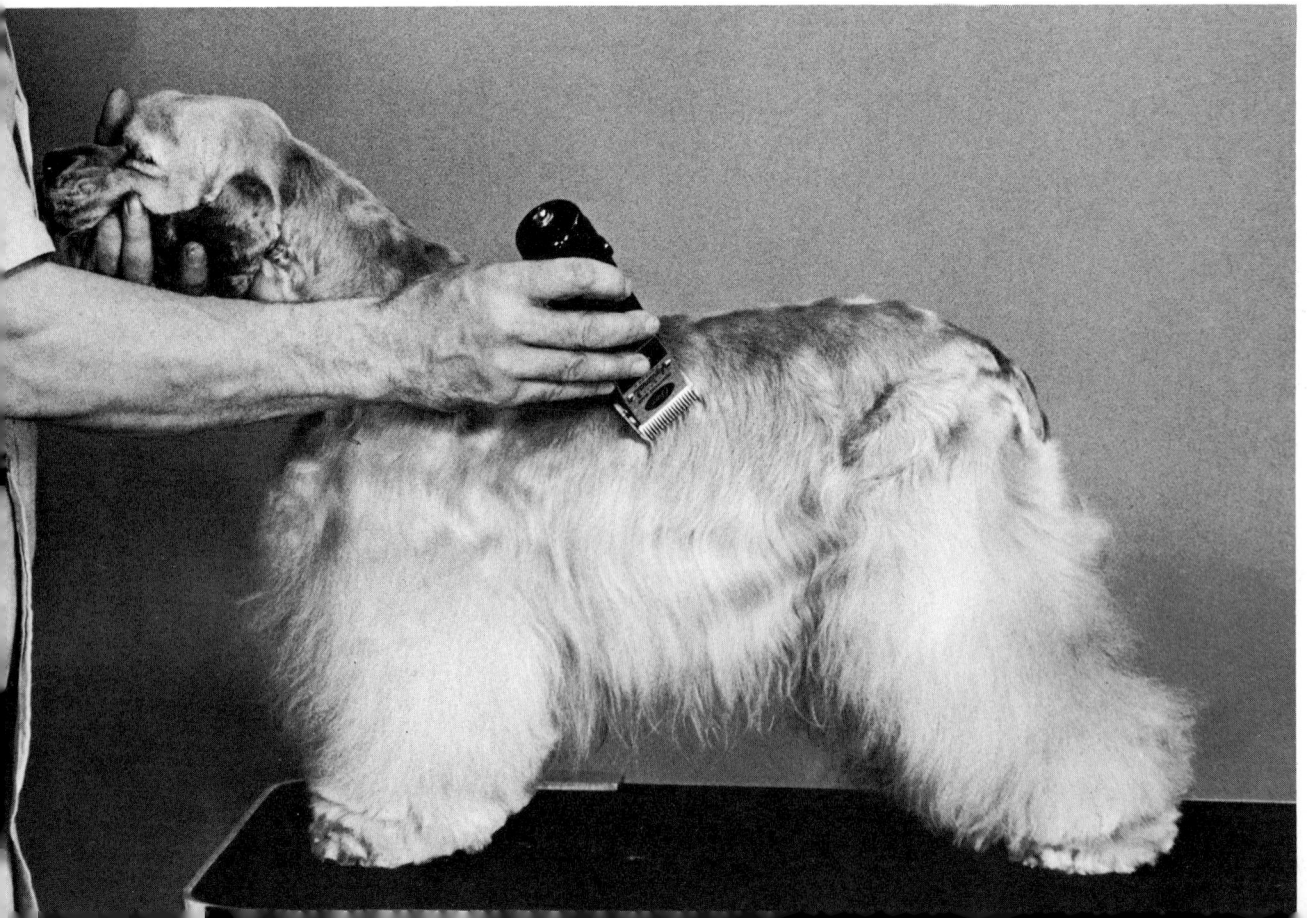

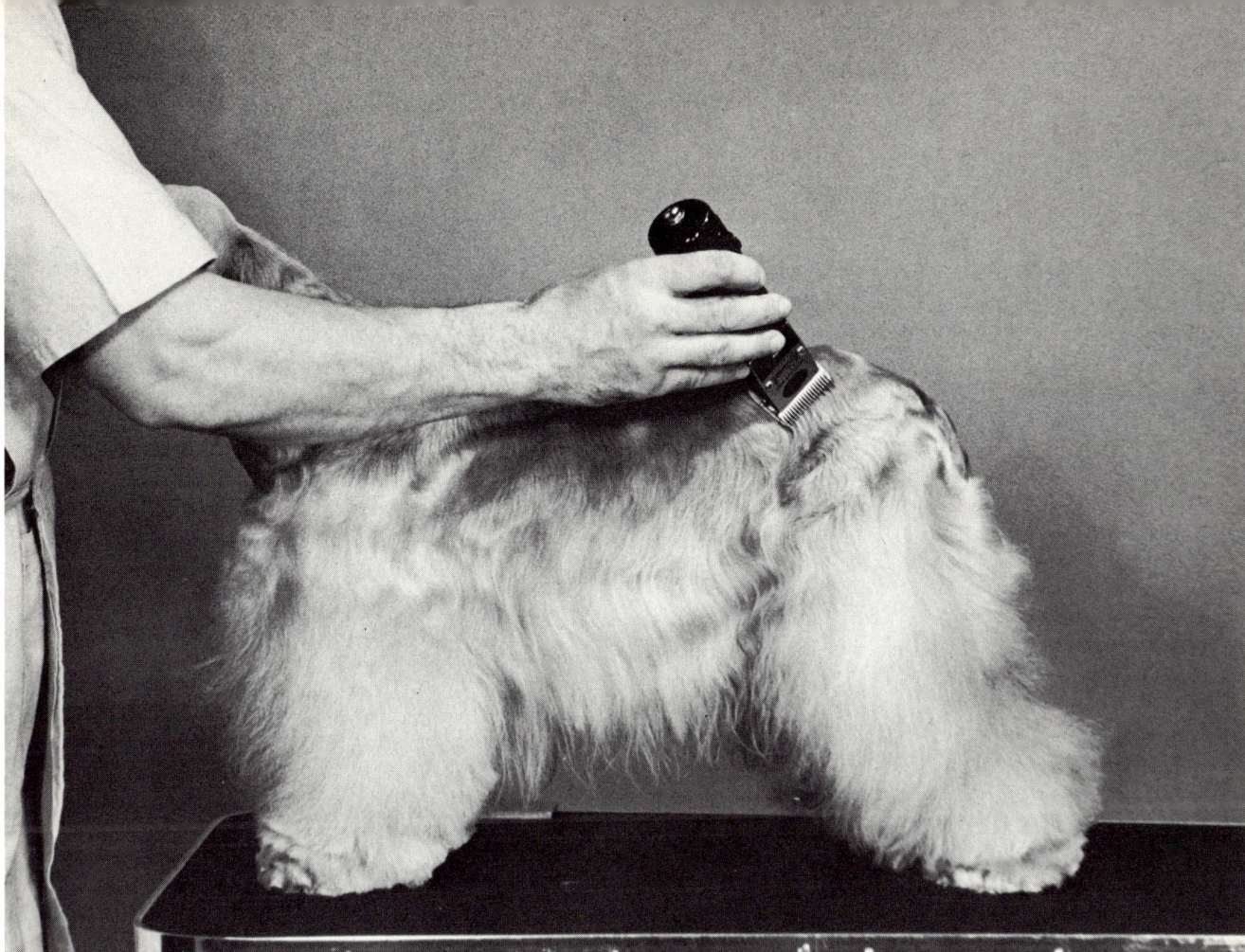

4-5. Clipping Hindquarters

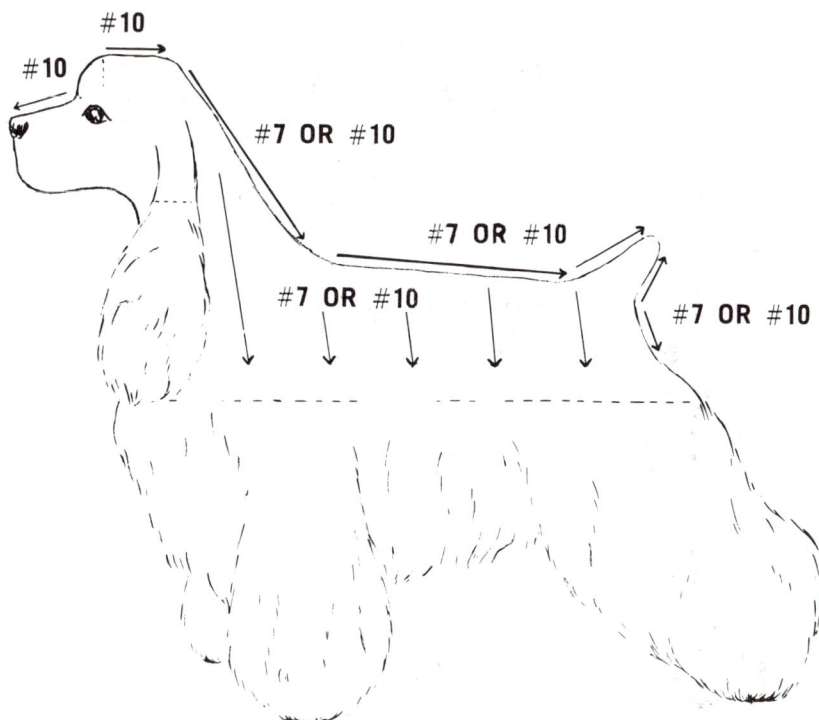

Diagram 2. American Cocker—Clipping Chart

Shaping and Blending

Brush out the feathering, and use a No. 7 blade or thinning shears to blend the body coat and feathering. Using the No. 7 blade as illustrated in *Photo 4-8*, shape and blend the clipped area into the feathering with the object of eliminating any line of demarcation between body and leg. This shaping and blending technique requires a very light, graceful stroke bringing the clippers into right angles with the body (*see Photo 4-9*).

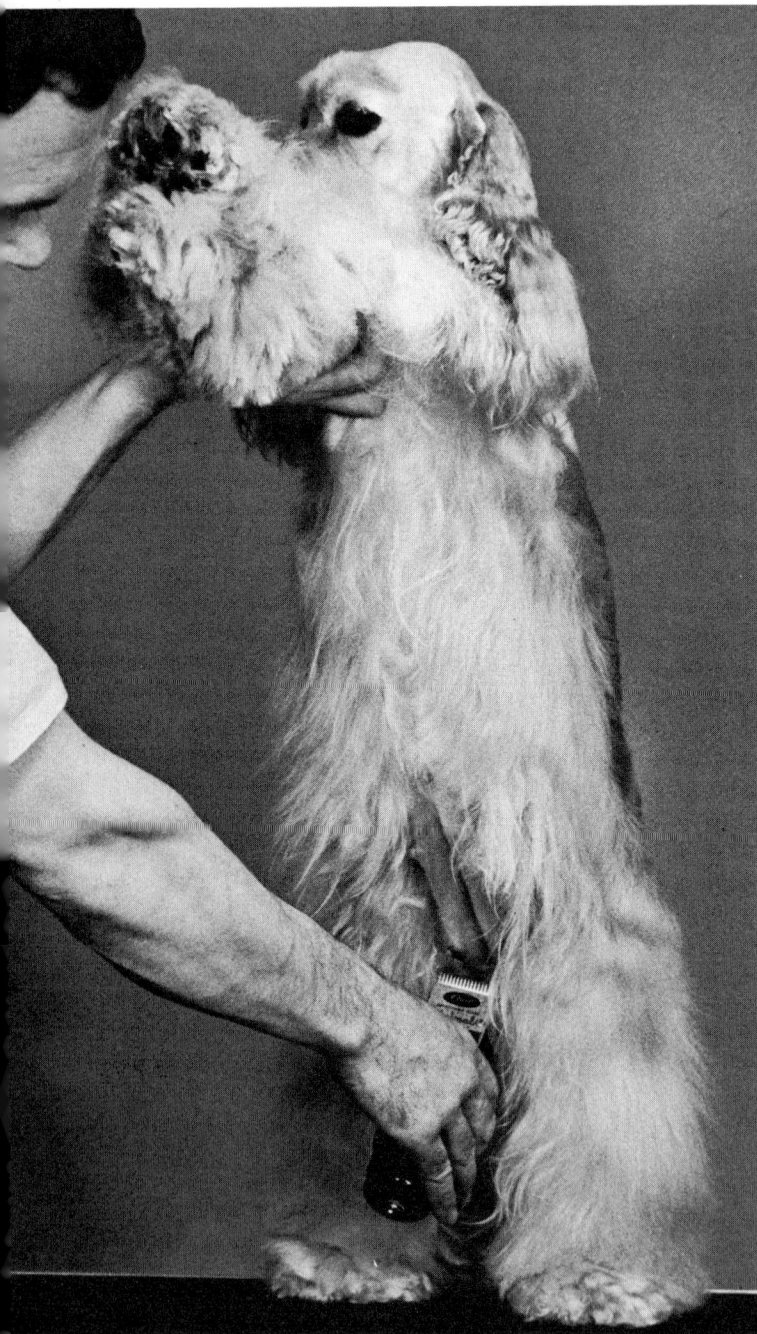

4-6. Clipping Tail

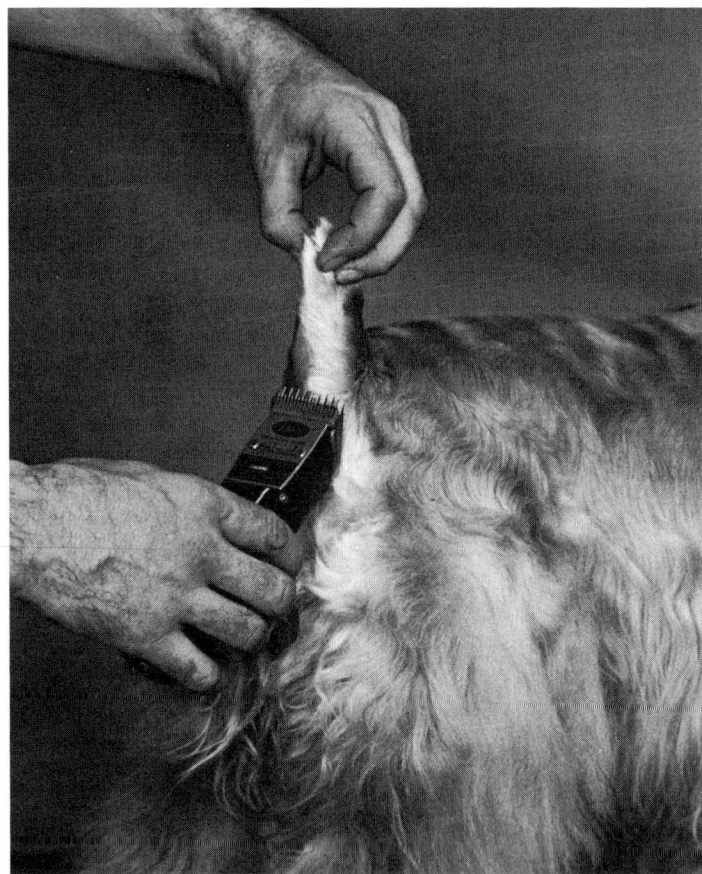

4-7. Clipping Stomach

4-8. Blending Body into Leg

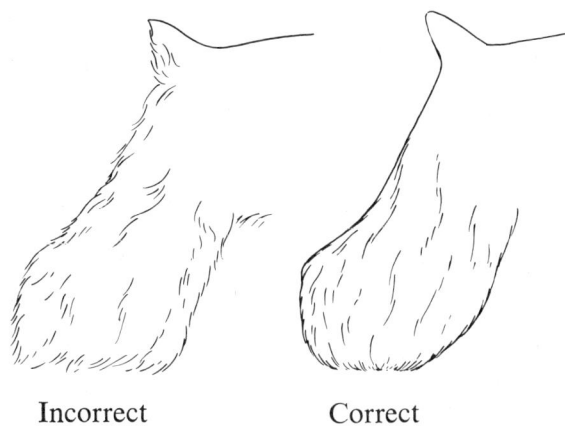

Incorrect   Correct

Diagram 3.   Tail and Leg—Rear

4-9. Clippers Held at Right Angles

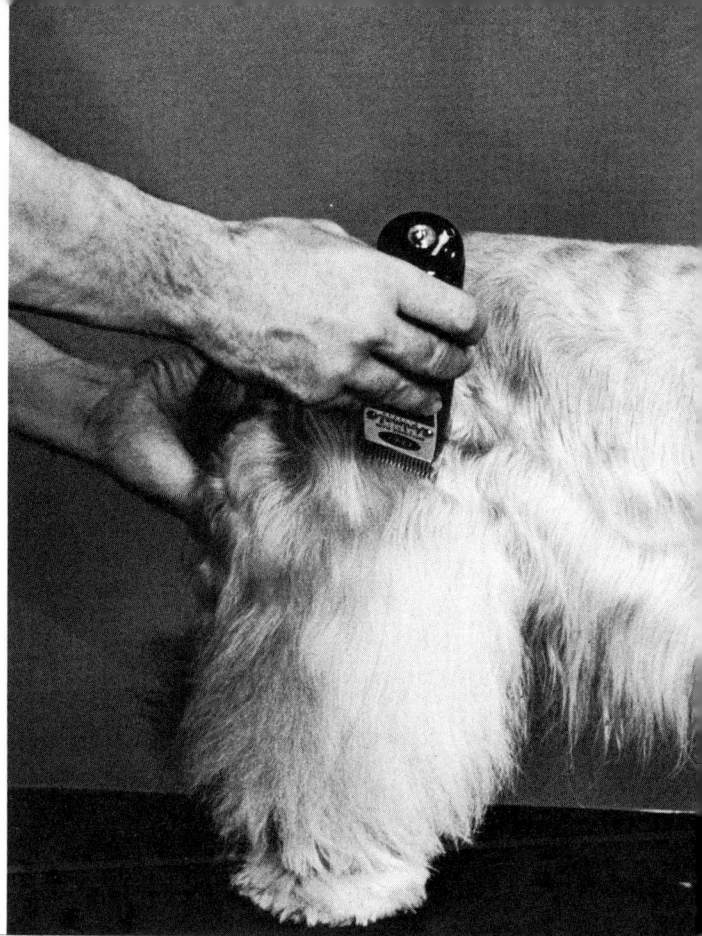

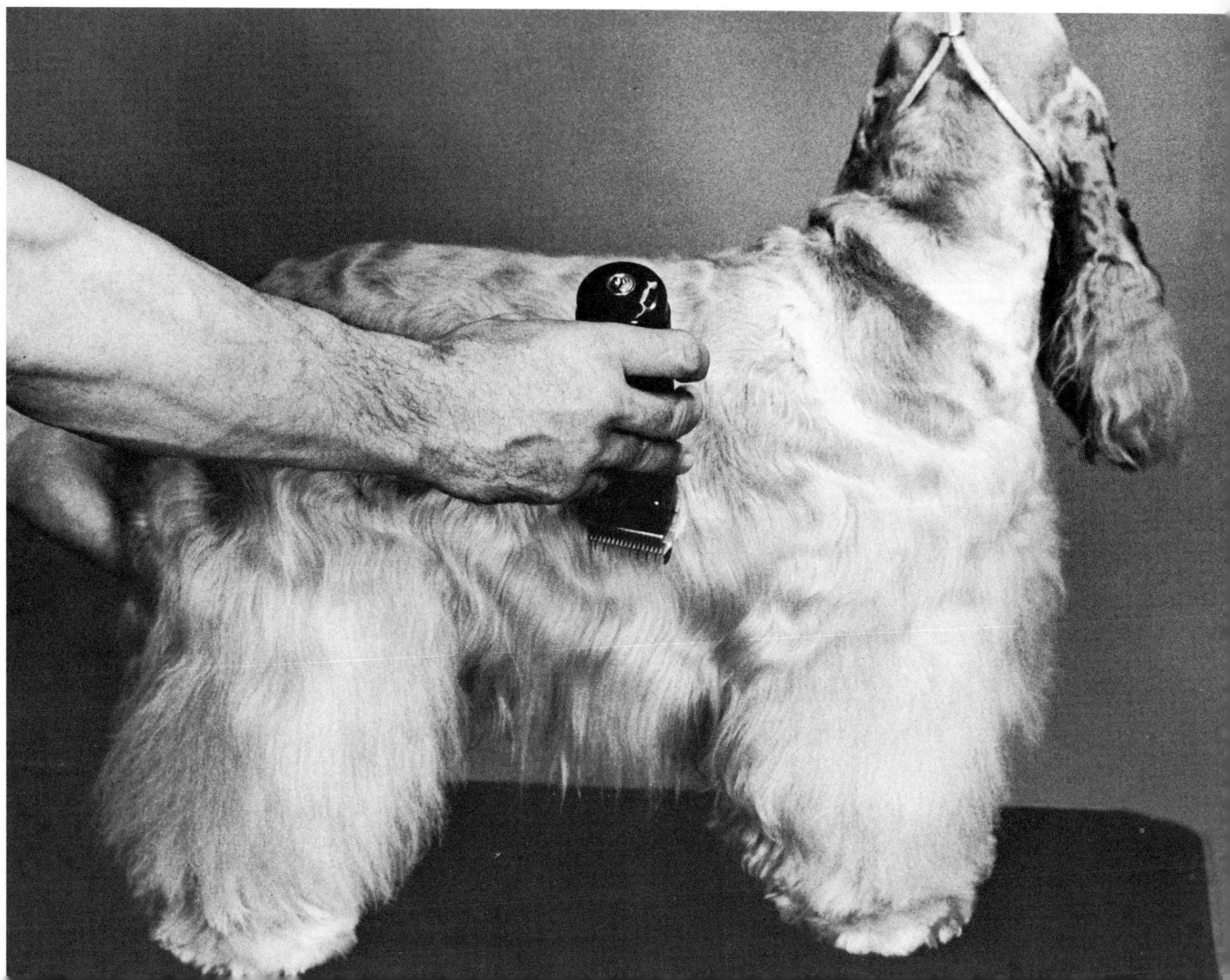

Ears, Head and Throat

When trimming these areas, it is advisable to clip the ears first so that the long hair around the base does not restrict your view while you are clipping the rest of the head. Use a No. 10 or No. 15 blade; start by working with the grain. If the coat texture is such that going with the grain does not give a clean enough appearance, you can always go over the area against the grain as necessary. Some breed varieties, especially the reds and buffs, show almost every clipper mark. This cannot be avoided, and although it may look unsightly for a short while, these marks will disappear within a week to ten days.

Clip both the inner and outer side of the ear one third of the way down. To do this most effectively, lay the ear flat on the palm of the hand. Clip the outer edge first. Then turn the ear over and do the underside, taking care to remove all the hair from around the ear canal (*Photos 4-10 and 4-11*).

Clip the head next, using either No. 10 or No. 15 blade, working with the grain. Standing at the front of the dog, holding the muzzle as illustrated, start clipping the top of the head about midway from the brow to the occiput, going back as far as the base of the skull (*Photo 4-12*). Leave a slight crown above the brow. Then clip the cheeks back to the corner of the ear (*Photo 4-13*). Clip around the ear to the lower edge of the base. Do this on both

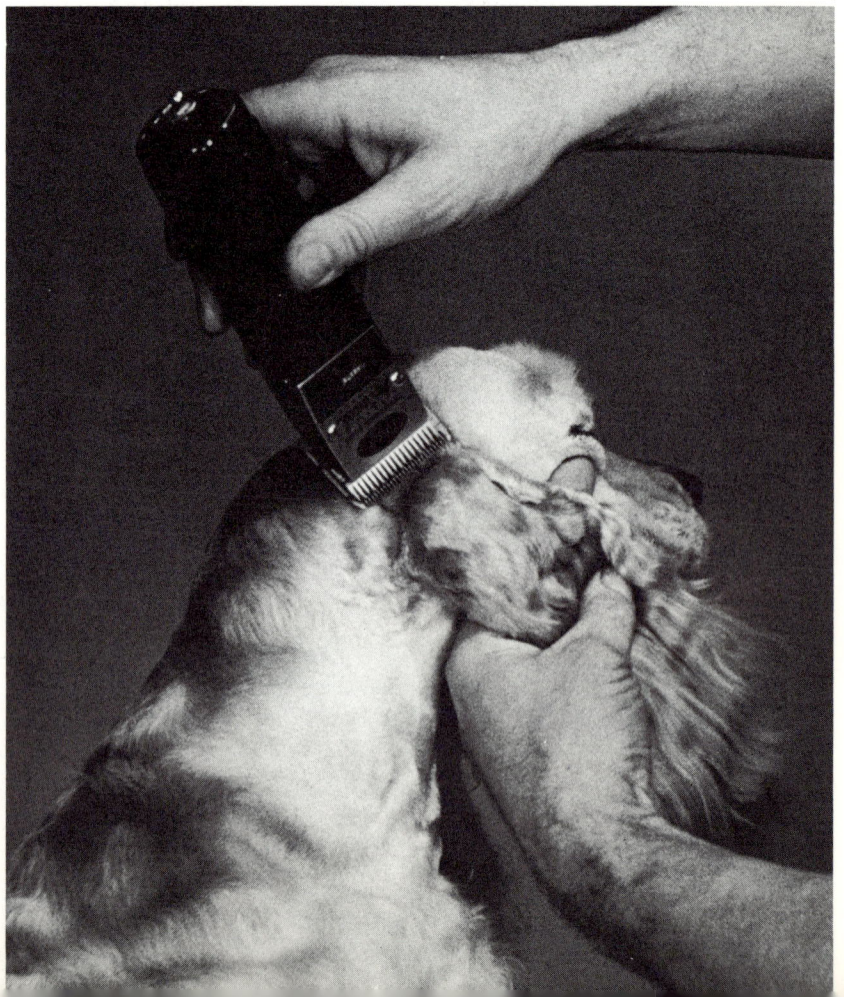

4-10. Clipping Outer Side of Ear

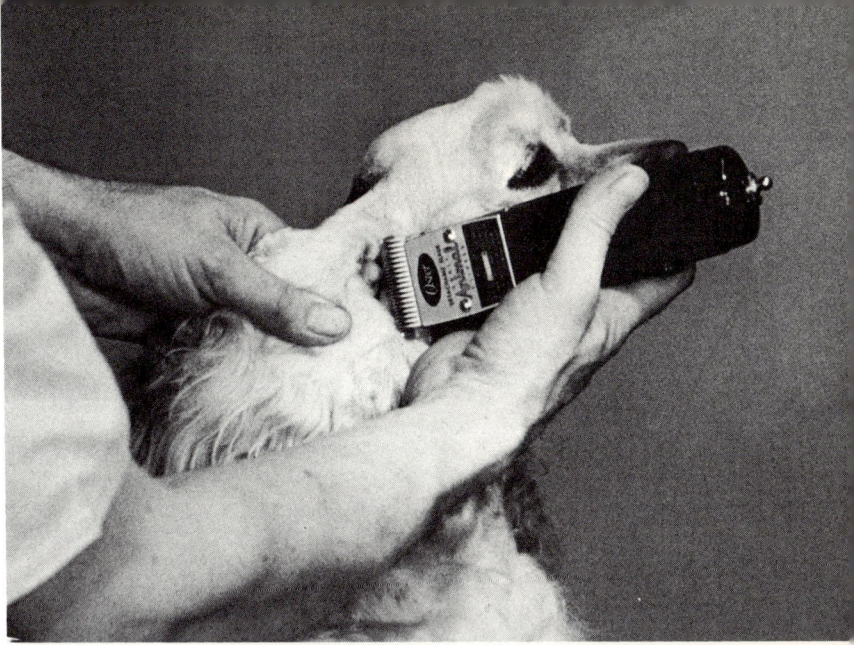

4-11. Clipping Inner Ear

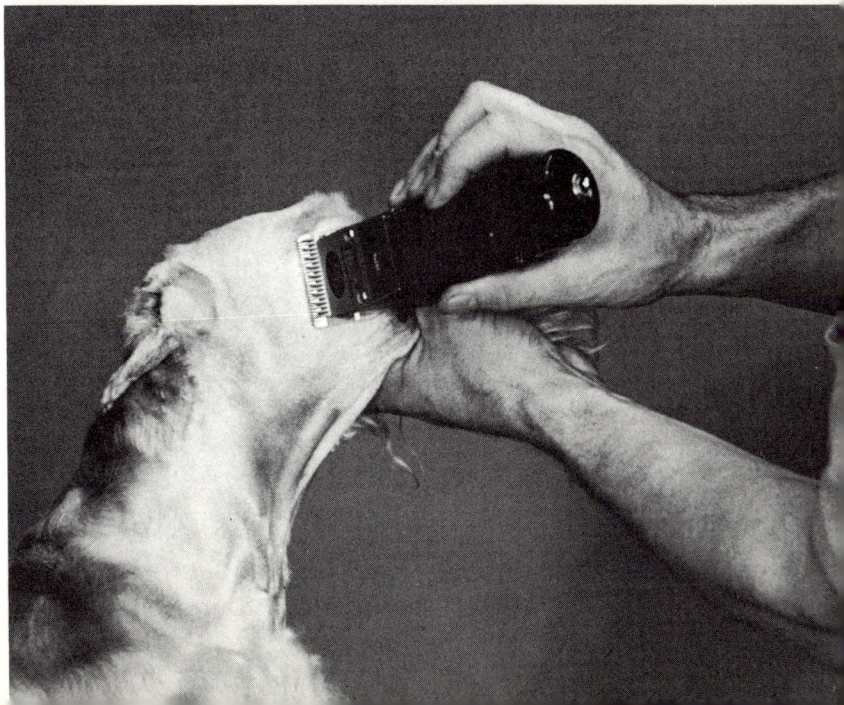

4-12. Clipping Skull

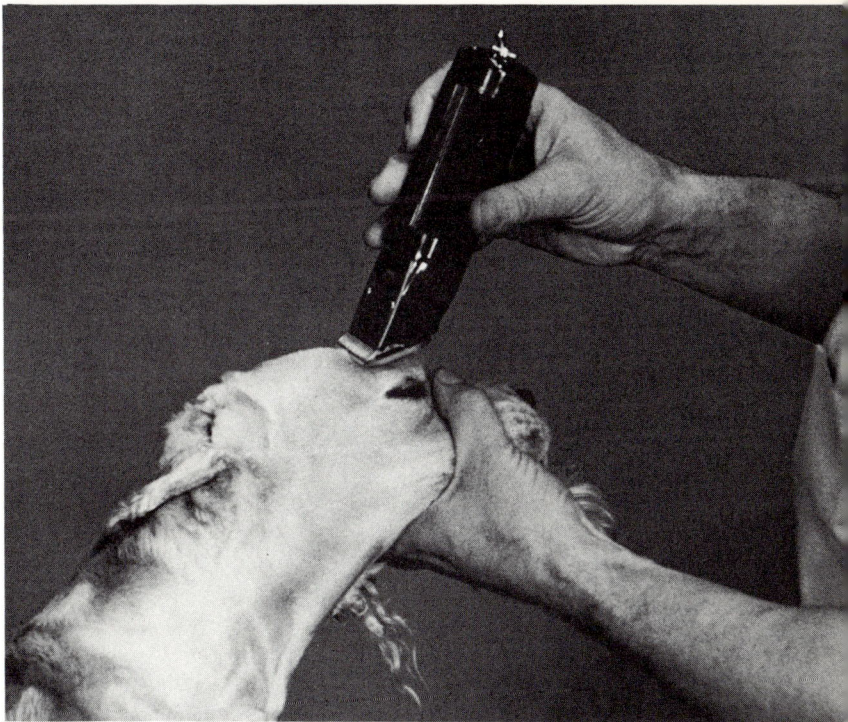

4-13. Clipping Cheeks

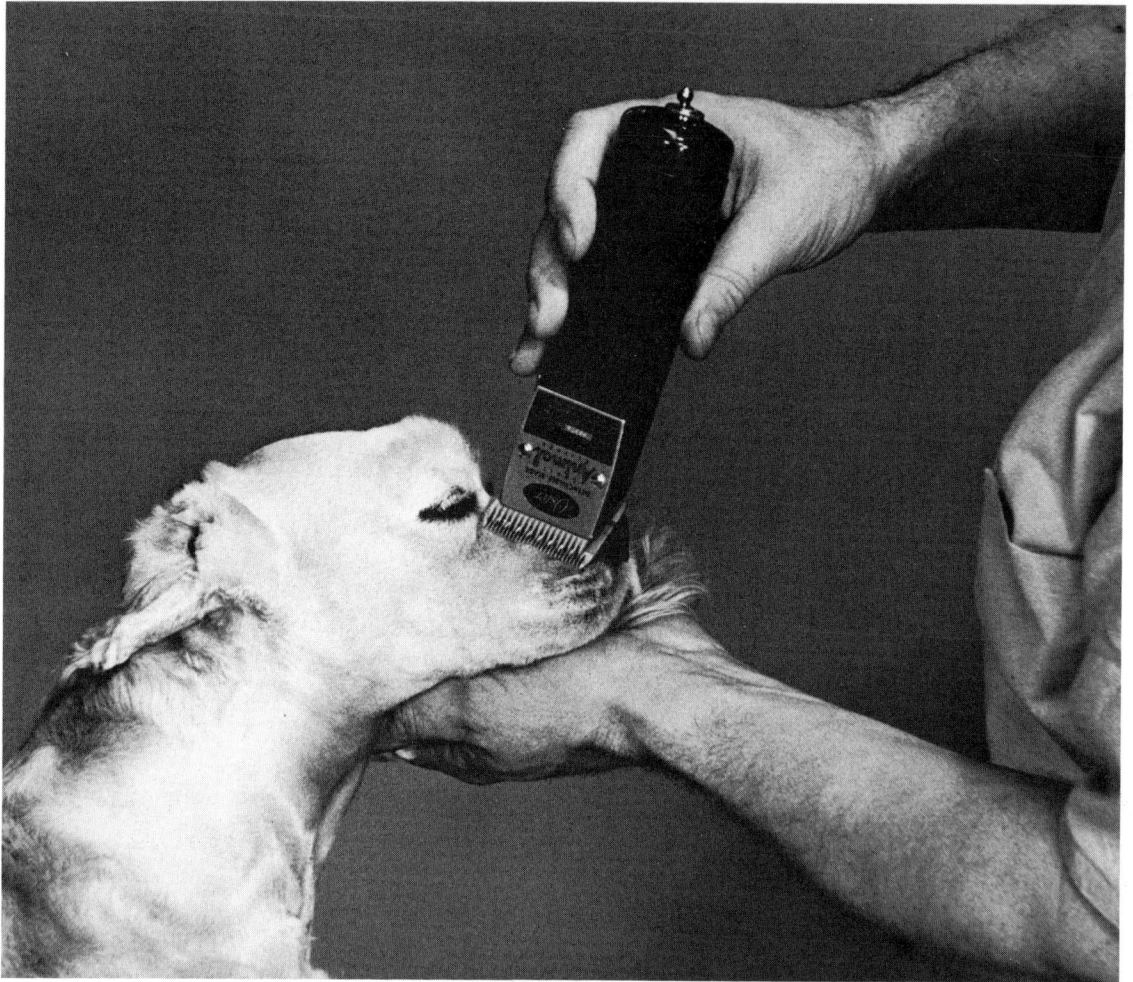

4-14. Clipping Side of Muzzle

sides. Clip the fore-face forward, against the grain, starting at the stop. Clip down the side of the muzzle to the lips, holding loose part of the lip on the palm of the hand (*Photo 4-14*). Clean out under the eyes, using a scooping motion. Clip the underjaw to the throat (*Photo 4-15*). Clean out the flews, gently stretching the lower lip backward. Next clip a deep U extending from the base of each ear down the throat and front of the neck and chest to the sternum (*Diagram 4*).

The area surrounding the closely clipped part of the throat should be blended smoothly with the longer hair of the chest (*Photo 4-16*).

34

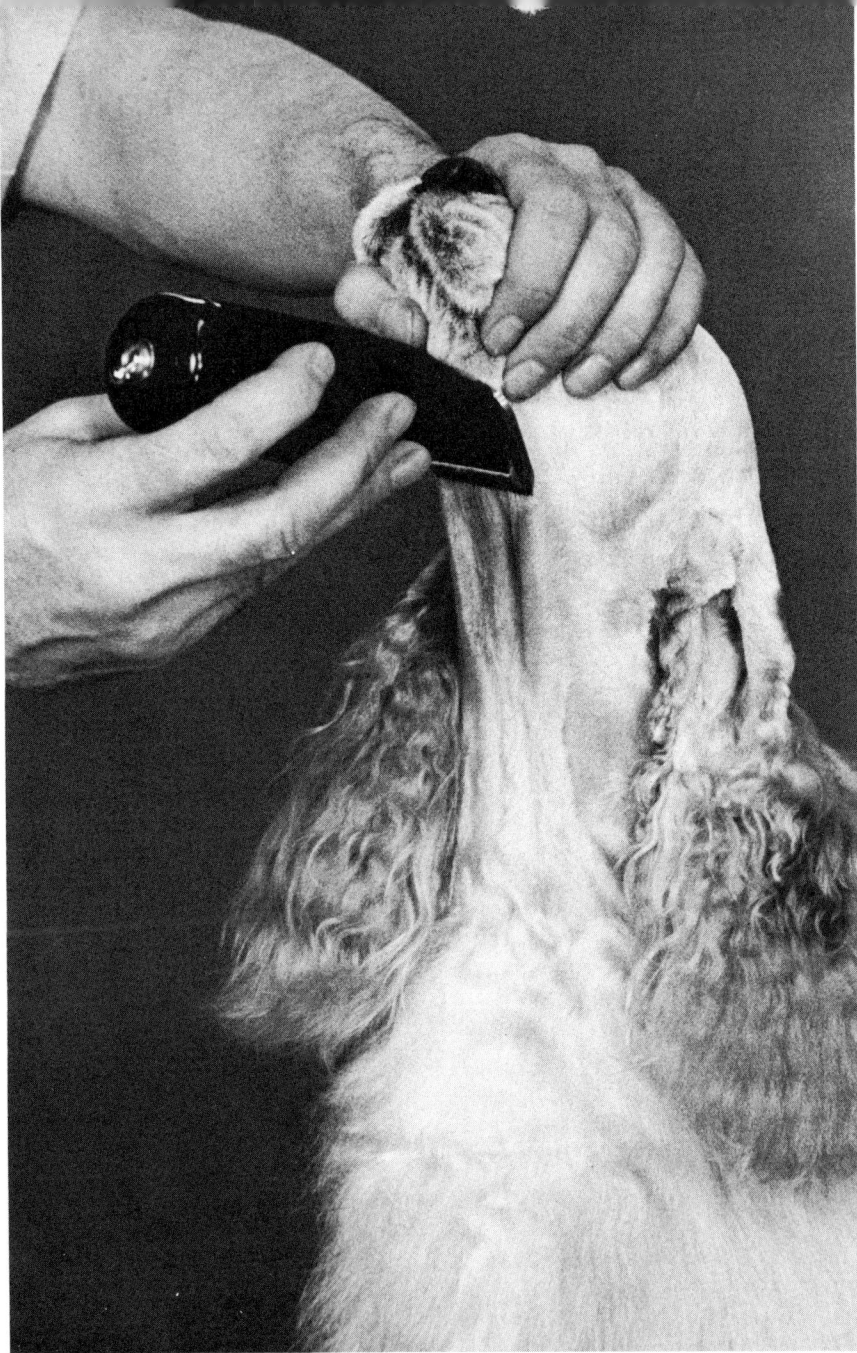

4-15.   Clipping the Throat

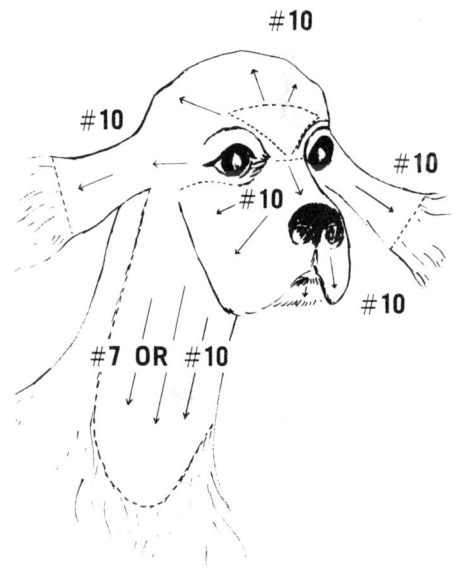

Diagram 4.
American Cocker—Head Chart

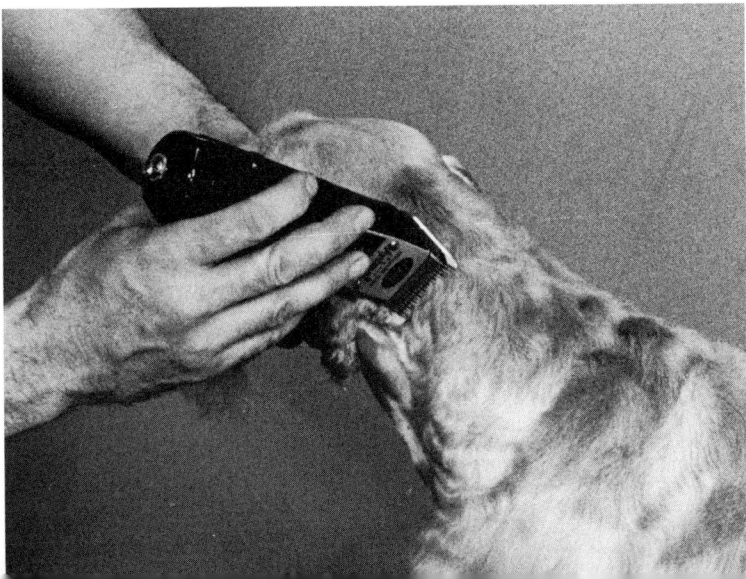

4-16.   Blending Neck and Chest

35

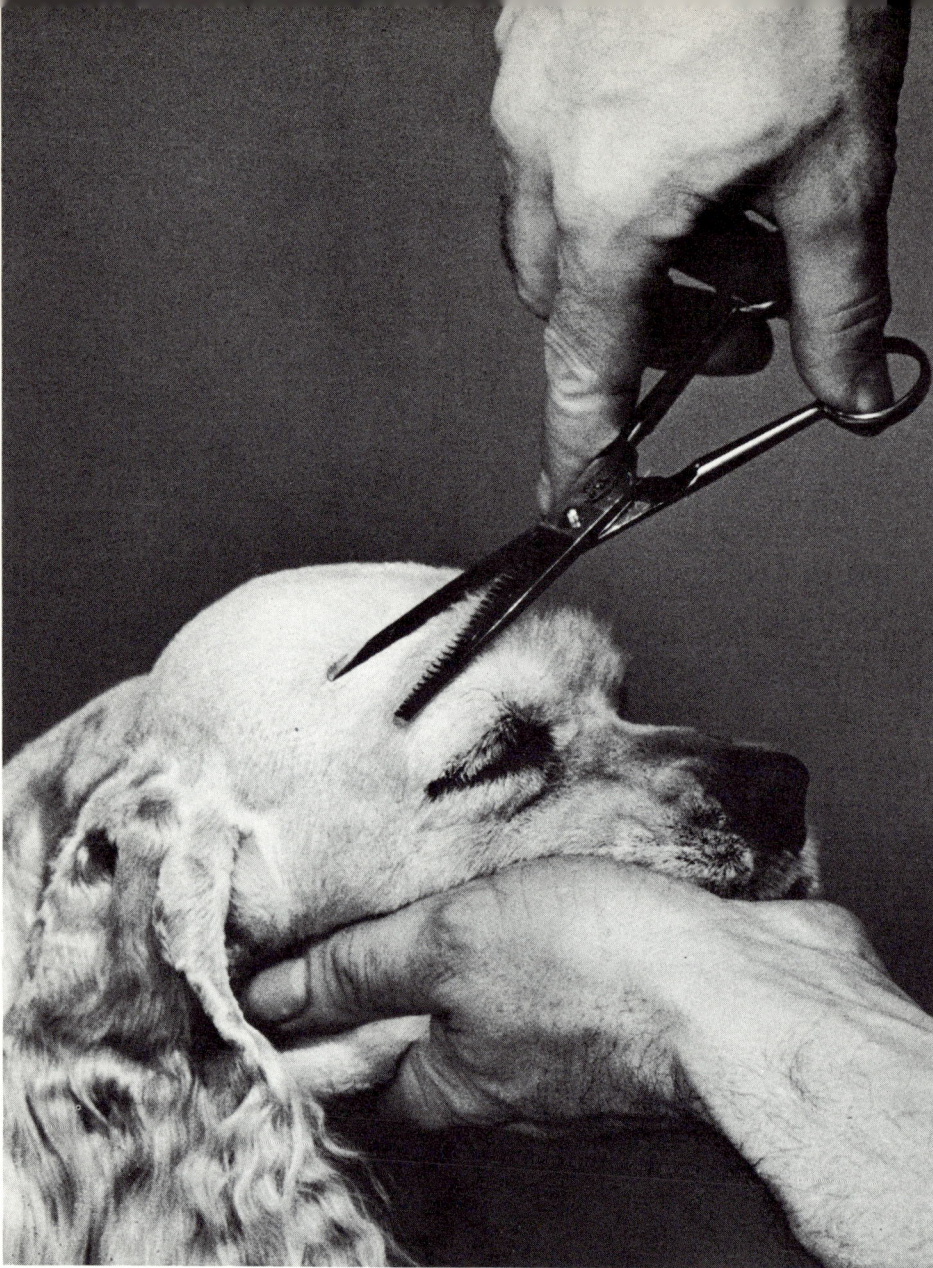

5-1. Blending Crown into Head

CHAPTER 5

SCISSORING

Head and Neck

The small crown over the brow must be blended with the thinning shears (*Photo 5-1*) so that the finished effect is that of a high forehead with a very pronounced stop. On those occasions when the hair on the head refuses to lie down, we have found that a coat dressing spray will often solve the problem.

Legs and Feet

The shoulders must be blended evenly with the leg feathering, avoiding harsh lines, and having as few undulations as is consistent with the texture of the coat. Front legs should be made to appear round, tapering out slightly toward the foot, taking on a bellshape effect.

Very little trimming is necessary to the front part of the leg. The hindquarters must also be blended, without noticeable definitions, from the top of the hips, over the thighs, past the hocks, to the feet. Scissoring should be done evenly with the contour of the leg, leaving the hair on the front slightly longer than on the back, to demonstrate good angulation (*Photo 5-2*). The inside as well as the outside of the legs should be evenly shaped and free from "bitty" ends in order to give the rear quarters a clean arch-like appearance. The hocks should be round and straight, to correspond with the front legs as much as possible (*Diagram 5*).

5-2. Scissoring Legs

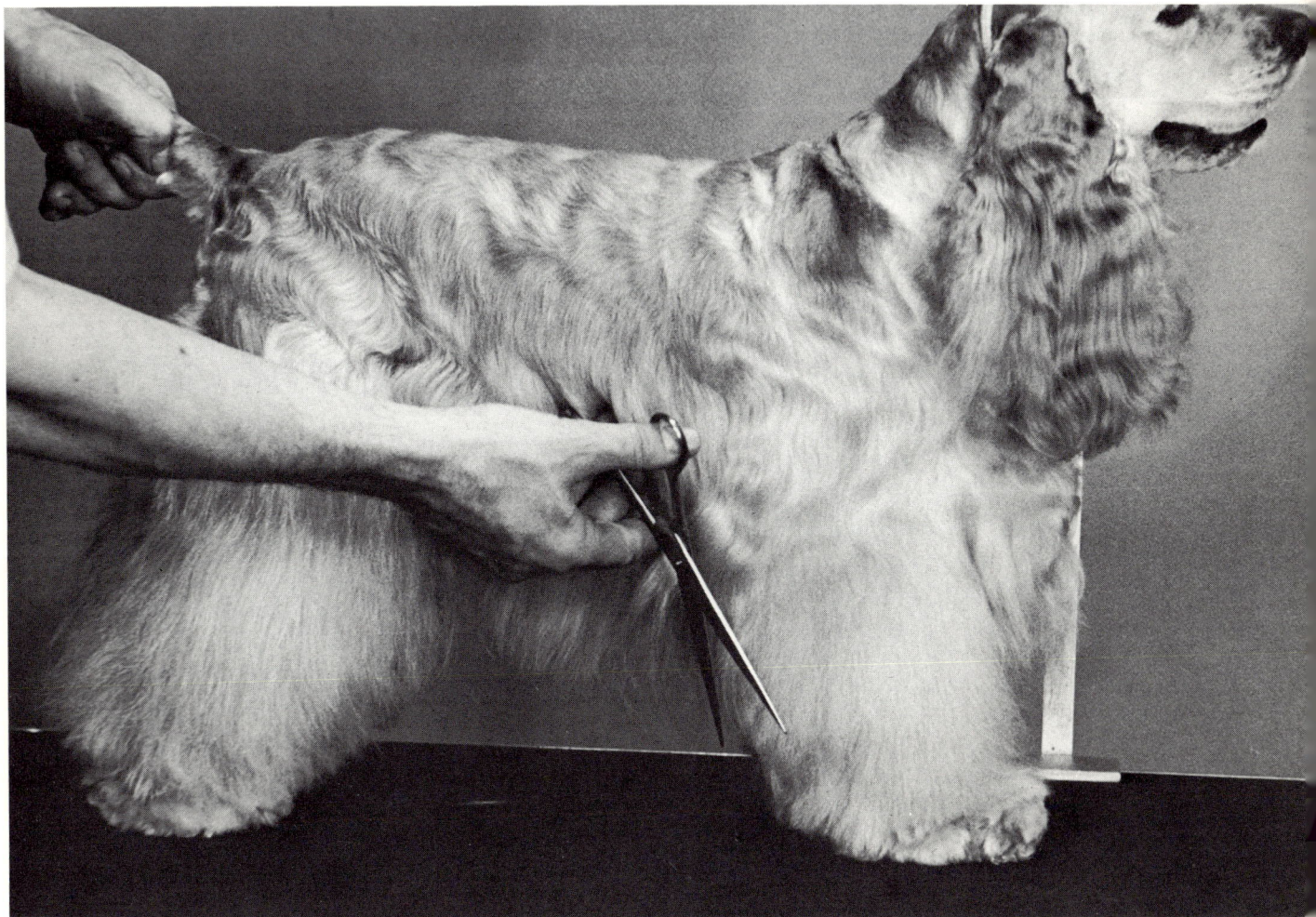

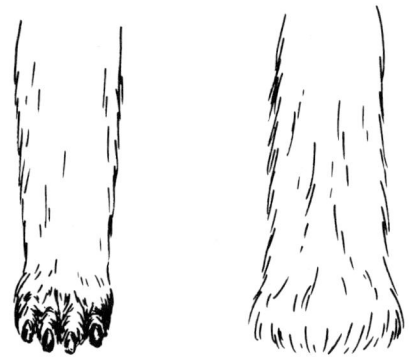

Diagram 6. Front Legs

Incorrect   Incorrect

Correct

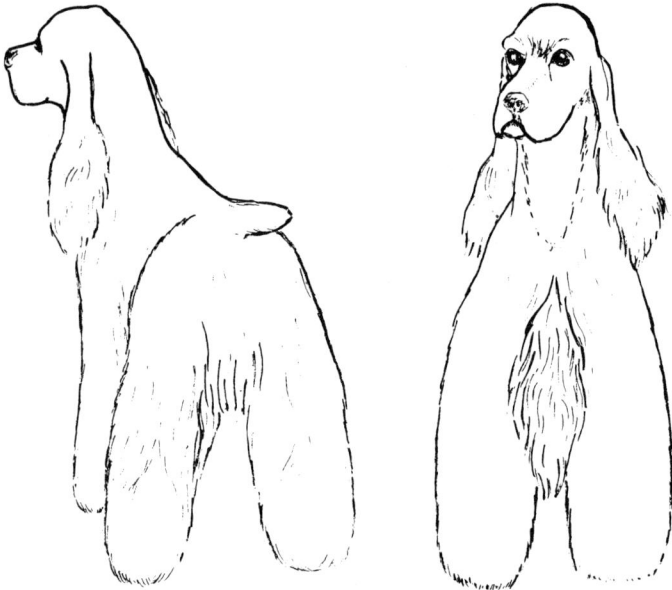

Diagram 5. Rear   Front

Grasp the lower part of the leg close to the foot, as you might hold a bunch of flowers, trim the hair level with the bottom of the foot. Shake the leg as if you were "shaking hands," and allow the dog to rest his weight on it. He can be encouraged to do so by raising the opposite foot. Brush the hair up all the way around the foot, shake the leg, and allow the dog to stand naturally. With the scissors held at an angle of approximately 45 degrees (*Photos 5-3 and 5-4*), scissor around the foot in as near to a perfect circle as the amount of feathering will allow, without exposing the nails.

Shake the leg again and trim off any loose ends that may appear. Repeat this final phase until the foot looks neat and round. If done correctly, the leg will be slightly bellshaped and convex at the foot. Neither toes nor nails should be visible (*Diagram 6*). Finish off by combing out any mats between the toes. Then, holding the foot as shown in *Photo 5-5*, scissor the hair from the pads.

38

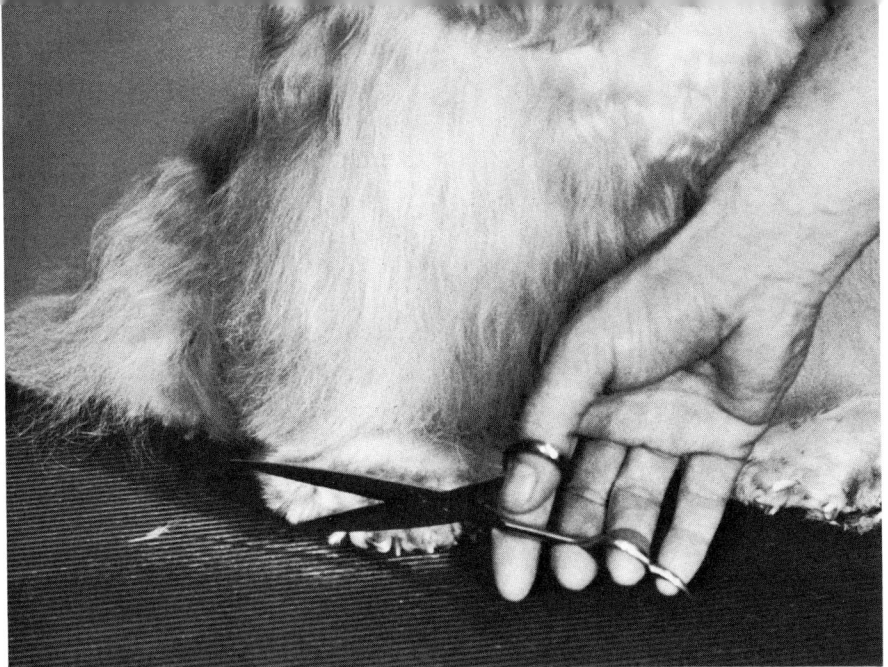

5-3. Scissoring around Foot

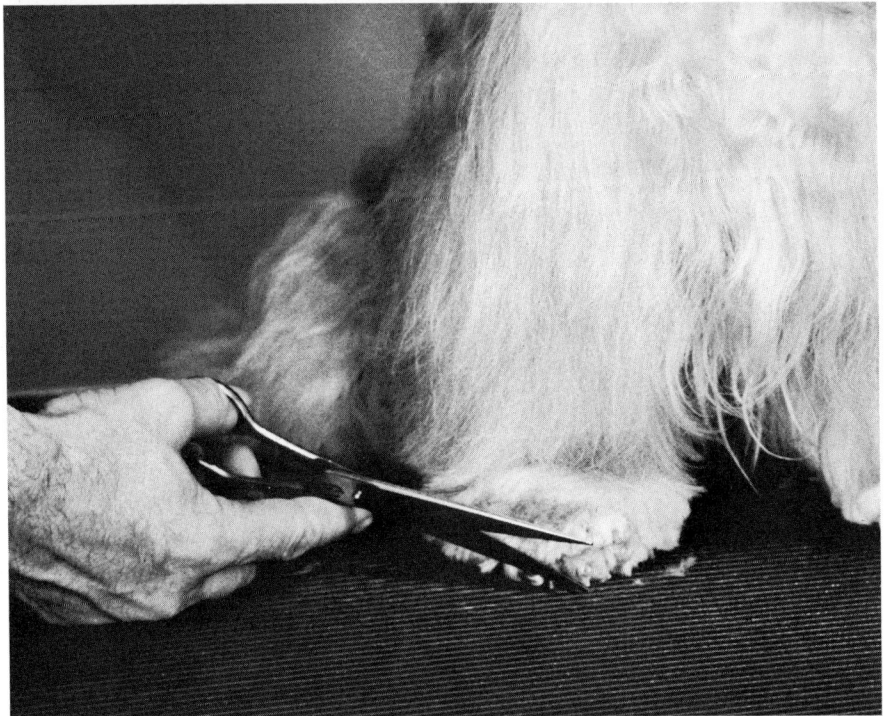

5-4. Scissoring around Foot

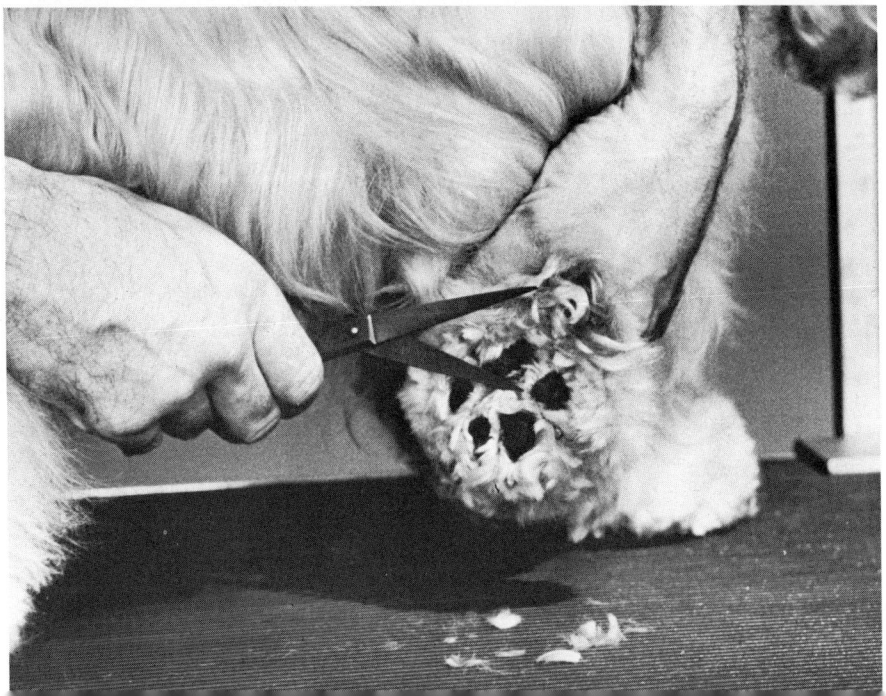

5-5. Scissoring Pads

Underchest

The hair on the underchest can be shortened if required. Scissor to follow the contour of the body, inclining gently from front to rear several inches below the body. To facilitate this maneuver, extend the front leg forward, bringing the elbow into right angle position, and scissor toward the rear along the line indicated (*Photo 5-6*). Repeat on opposite side. Scissors may be used, but thinning shears give the best results.

Finish

If the above instructions are followed in a systematic and methodical fashion, the end result should bear a reasonable resemblance to a Cocker trimmed for show (*Photo 5-7*).

5-6.   Scissoring Underchest

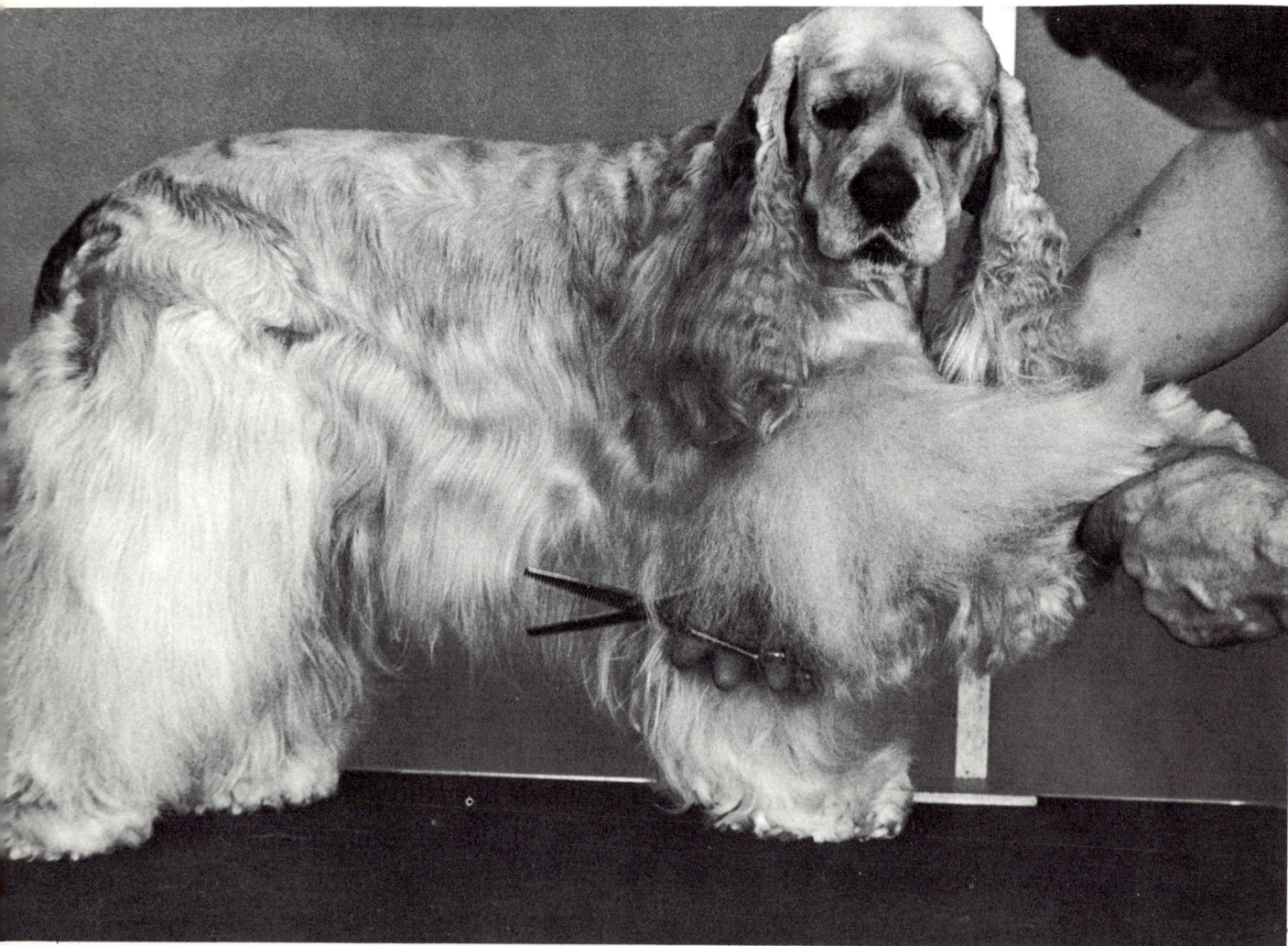

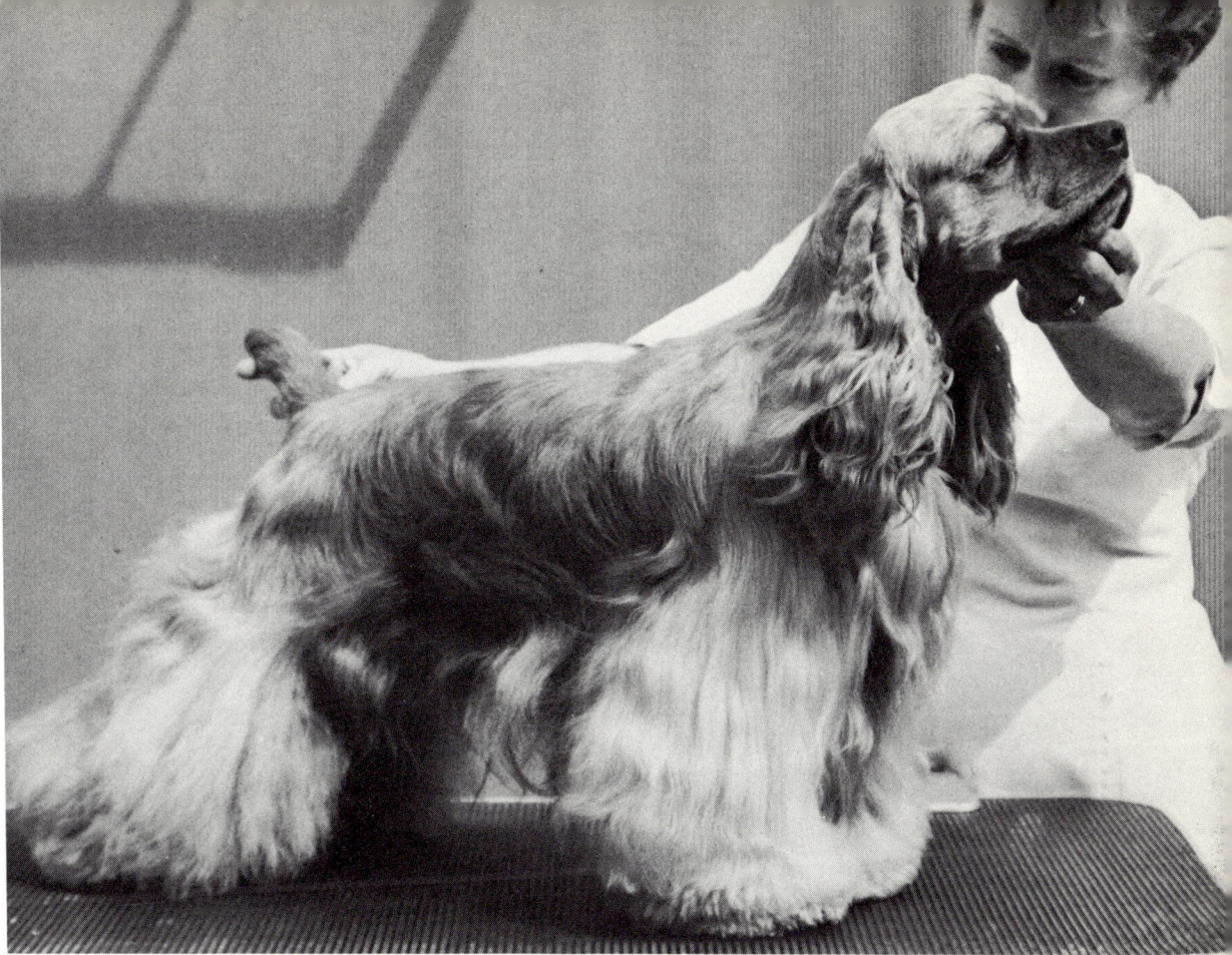

5-7.   Finish

5-8.   American Cocker Show Dog

PART II

Grooming For Show

CHAPTER 6

SHOW GROOMING

There are so many aspects involved in preparing the various spaniels and setters for show that a completely detailed step-by-step procedure would require a separate book for each major breed. For the purposes of this book we have tried to give general guide lines and concentrate on basic fundamentals to help the beginner establish the foundation for grooming any of the individual breeds in the Sporting Group.

If you are going to prepare a show dog successfully you must become a combination hairdresser and makeup artist. Ample consideration must be given to the conformation of the dog, so as to exploit its maximum show potential. Faults can be minimized and virtues accentuated by expert grooming. These important points should be considered before work on the dog is actually begun. A thorough knowledge of the breed you are going to work on is essential. Read the Breed Standard. Attend dog shows. Make a habit of seeing winners in the show ring. Watch the professional handlers at work at the shows putting on the finishing touches. If you approach the handlers at the right time, they'll be glad to answer your questions.

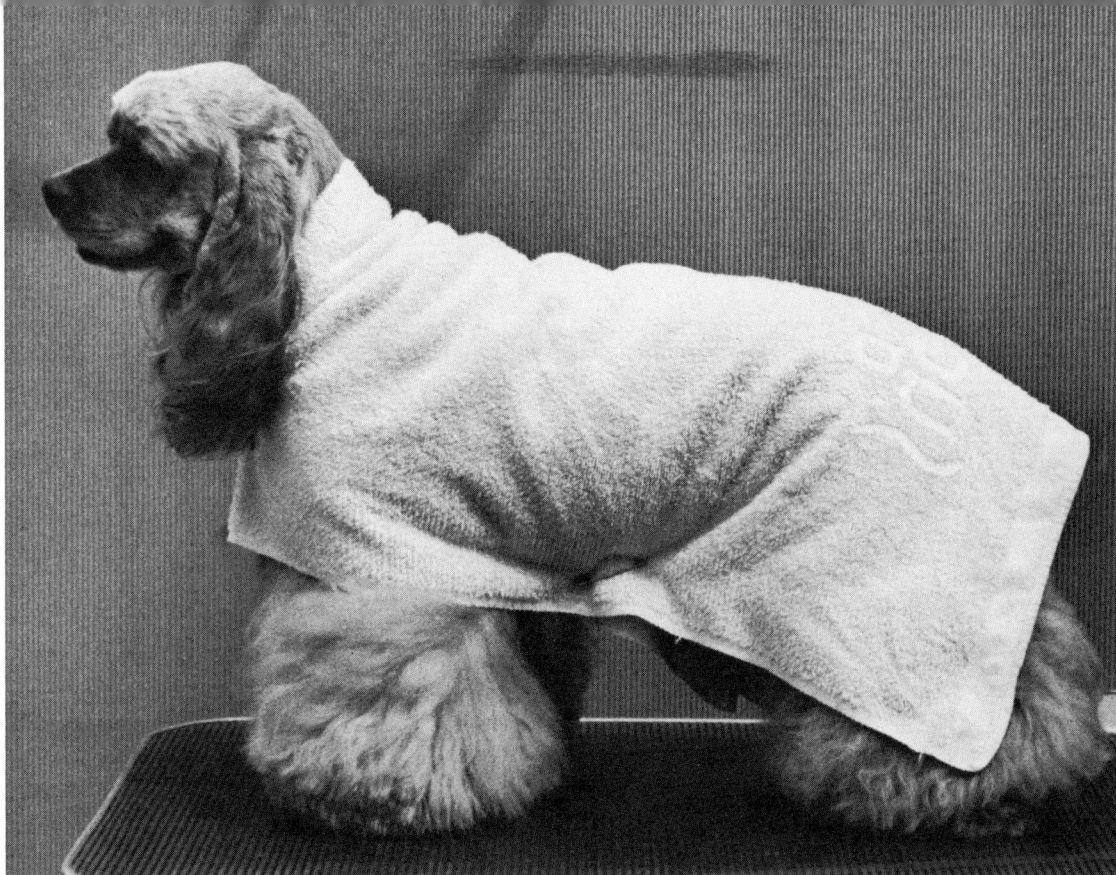

6-1. Sacking

Sacking

In preparing your dog for show it is not necessary to dwell on the grooming fundamentals again such as brushing and bathing. It would simply be a repetition of the techniques described in the pet section. The only exception or addition worth noting in preparing a dog for show is the need for "sacking" the dog after the bath. This helps to flatten the coat which is much to be desired. It is accomplished by folding a bath towel in half, draping it over the dog's back, and pinning it in front of the chest and under the belly (*Photo 6-1*). Place the dog in a warm, confined area until he is completely dry. Then the coat must be brushed out again with a pin brush.

Most serious Cocker exhibitors would be horrified at the idea of using clippers on any area beyond the head and neck, but it is possible to use the clippers on various parts of the body without ill effect. However, because this practice tends to make certain types of coats curl up, thus reducing your dog's chances of winning against more professionally "put down" competition, it is not recommended for the serious exhibitor.

THE THINNING SHEARS

When we talk about grooming the Spaniel and Setter for show, we are talking mainly about the use of the thinning shears. The use of thinning shears instead of clippers is the big and important difference between show and pet grooming. It is an art and cannot be mastered overnight. The function of the thinning shears is to trim the coat without leaving noticeable ridges or "bitty" curled up ends. The thinning shears differ mainly from regular scissors in that they cut with a feathering effect rather than a straight, sharp cutting effect.

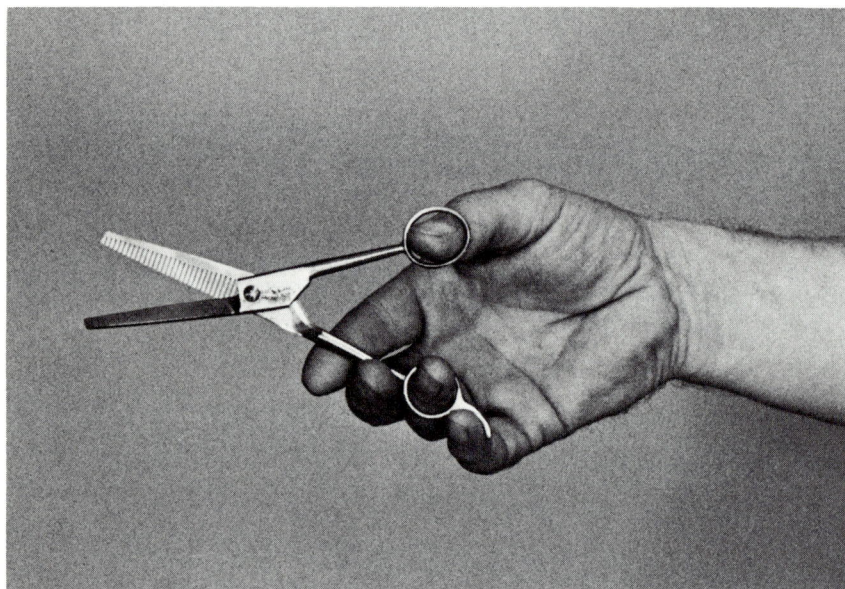

6-2. Thinning Shears Technique

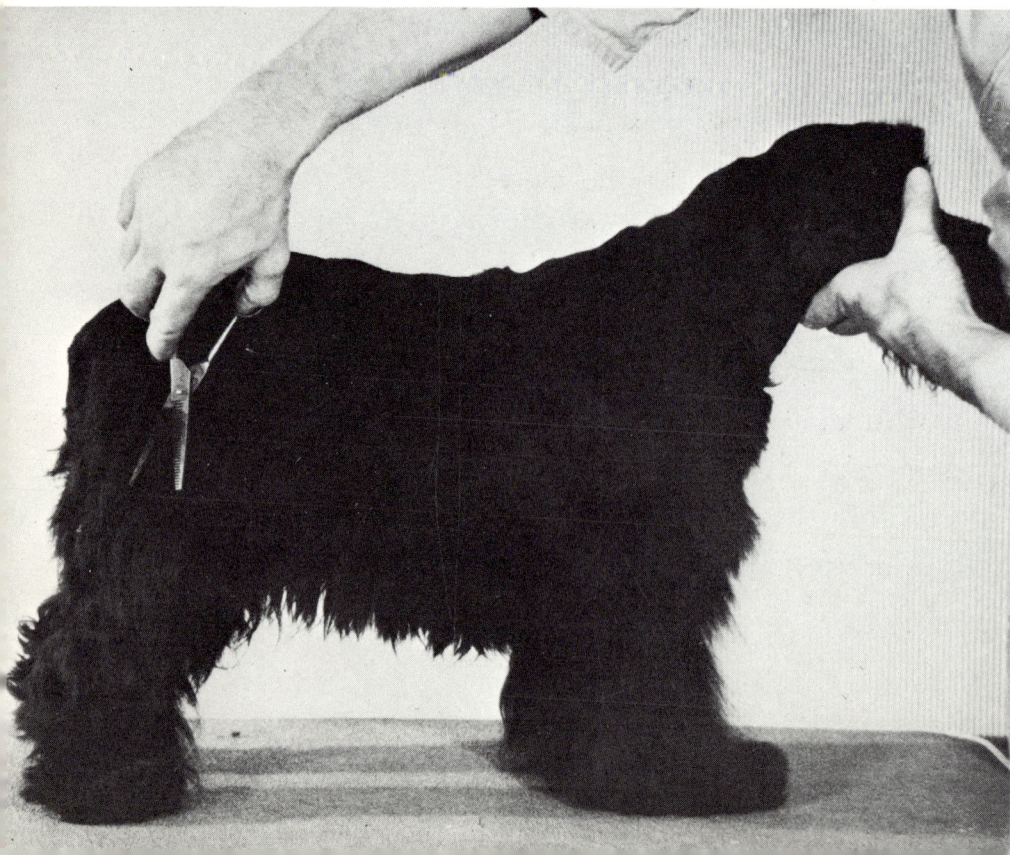

6-3. Trimming with Lay of Coat

Photo by Mario Migliorini

It may help you to master the technique of using the thinning shears if you devote some time to their proper handling. It will take practice and patience. First, hold the shears firmly with your little finger hooked over the open shank, the tip of your fourth finger through the finger hold, and your third finger resting on the handle. Your index finger is used to brace the shears, and the tip of your thumb goes into the thumb hole (*Photo 6-2*).

Cut by holding the lower section of the shears as steadily as possible, working mainly with your thumb. The thinning shears are always used with the lay of the coat, following the contour of the body. They should always be held vertically (*Photo 6-3*) never horizontally or across the coat.

Head, Ears and Throat

If you are doing a Cocker show trim, proceed as described under pet clip. See *Diagram 4* for the Head, Ears, and Throat, which are clipped in identical fashion for pet or show trim.

The crown must be blended with the clipped portion of the fore-skull and should lie flat (*See Photo 4-18, Ch. 4*). If an unruly crown cannot be controlled by a liberal amount of coat dressing, it can be taped down with masking tape while it is still wet and then dried with a drier. When the tape is removed the hair should be in perfect position.

45

Diagram 7. American Cocker—Center of Back

Trimming the Body

With the trimming shears, start from the base of the skull and trim the neck to look slightly arched (*Photo 6-4*). Trim the hair shorter at the base, gradually increasing the length at the withers so as to blend the neck cleanly into the shoulder. The shoulders and hips (*Photo 6-5*) must be thinned from the top to blend smoothly with the feathering, always avoiding harsh lines and having as few undulations as is consistent with the texture of the coat.

The area surrounding the closely clipped part of the throat should blend smoothly with the apron.

The area in the center of the back, between the two unshaded areas of *Diagram 7* should be thinned from underneath so as not to appear bulky. Thinning from underneath leaves the body coat long, giving the impression that the coat in the middle is draped over the dog's back like a shawl.

Legs and Feet

The hindquarters must also be blended without noticeable definitions from the top of the hips over the thighs, past the hocks to the feet. Scissoring should be done evenly with the contour of the leg, leaving the hair on the front slightly longer than on the back, to demonstrate good angulation. The inside as well as the outside of the legs should be evenly shaped, giving the rear quarters a clean, arch-like appearance. The hocks should be round and straight to correspond with the front legs as much as possible. (*See Diagram 5* and Legs and Feet Section under Pet Trimming).

The tail should be thinned to taper gently from the base to the tip on all sides. The rectal area should be trimmed close but made to blend (*Photo 6-6*).

6-4. Trimming Neck   6-5. Trimming Shoulders and Hips

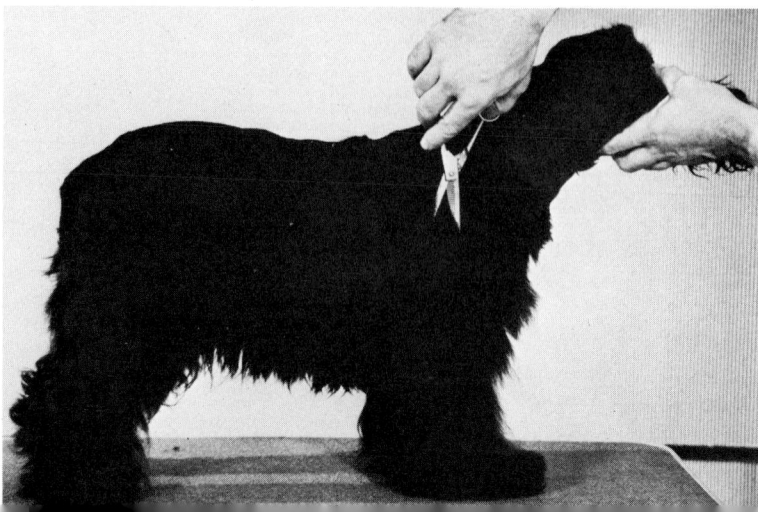

Photo by Mario Migliorini

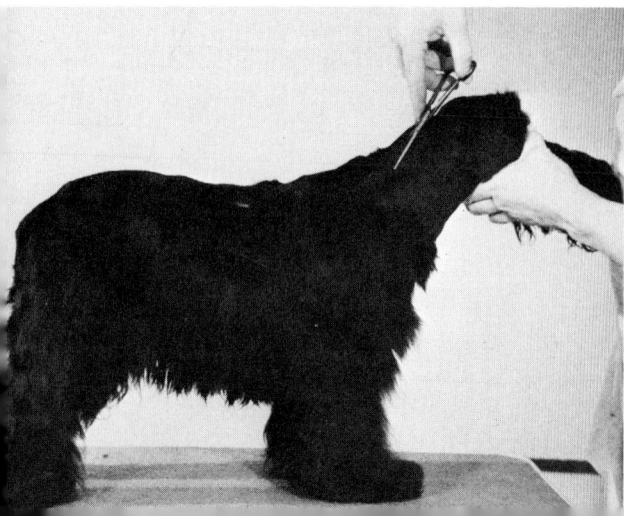

Photo by Mario Migliorini

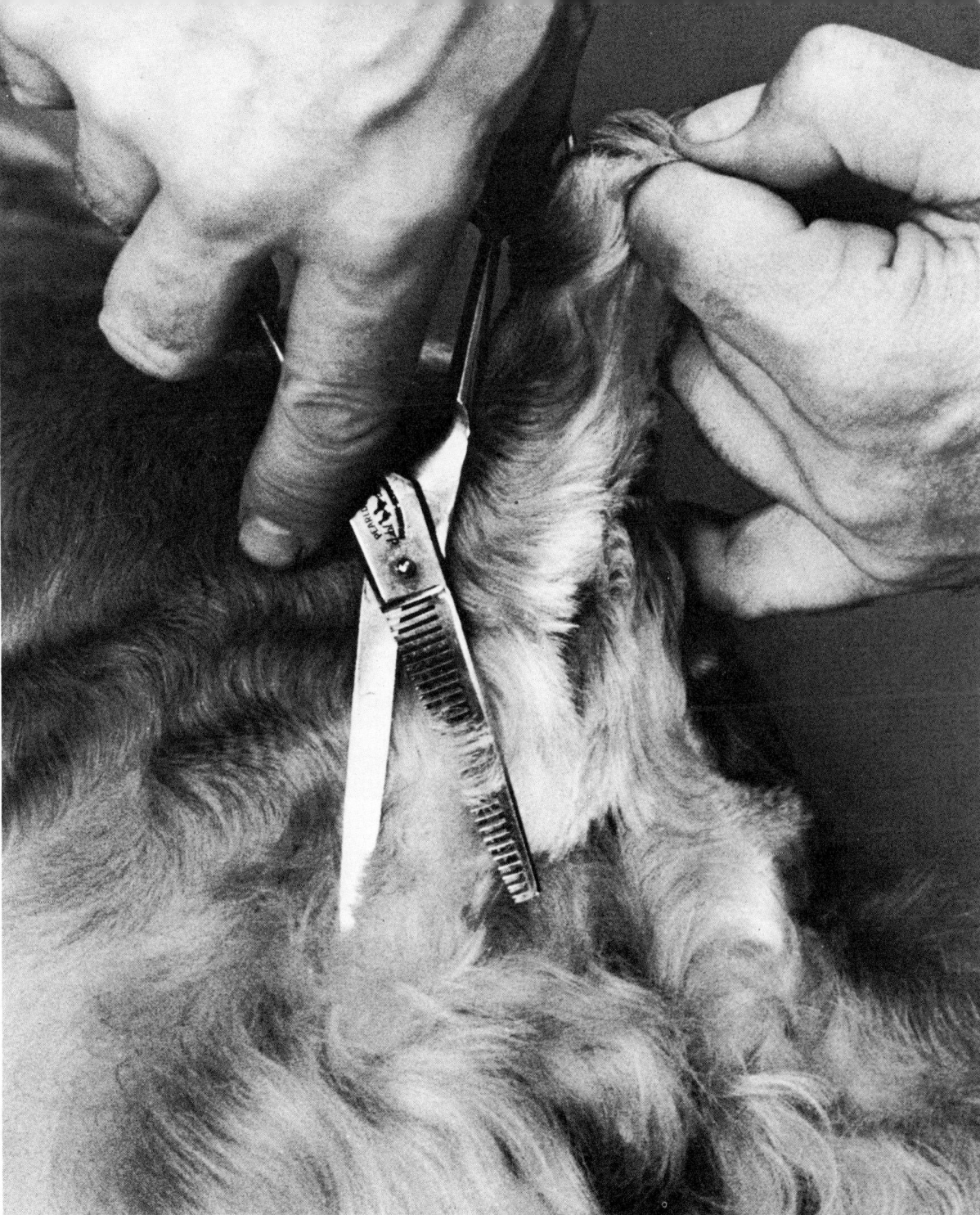

6-6. Trimming Rectal Area

All parts of the coat that are trimmed must blend smoothly with the surrounding areas to look as natural as possible. To obtain the best effect, start grooming your Cocker at least 10 days before the show to allow time for any unevenness of coat to grow out.

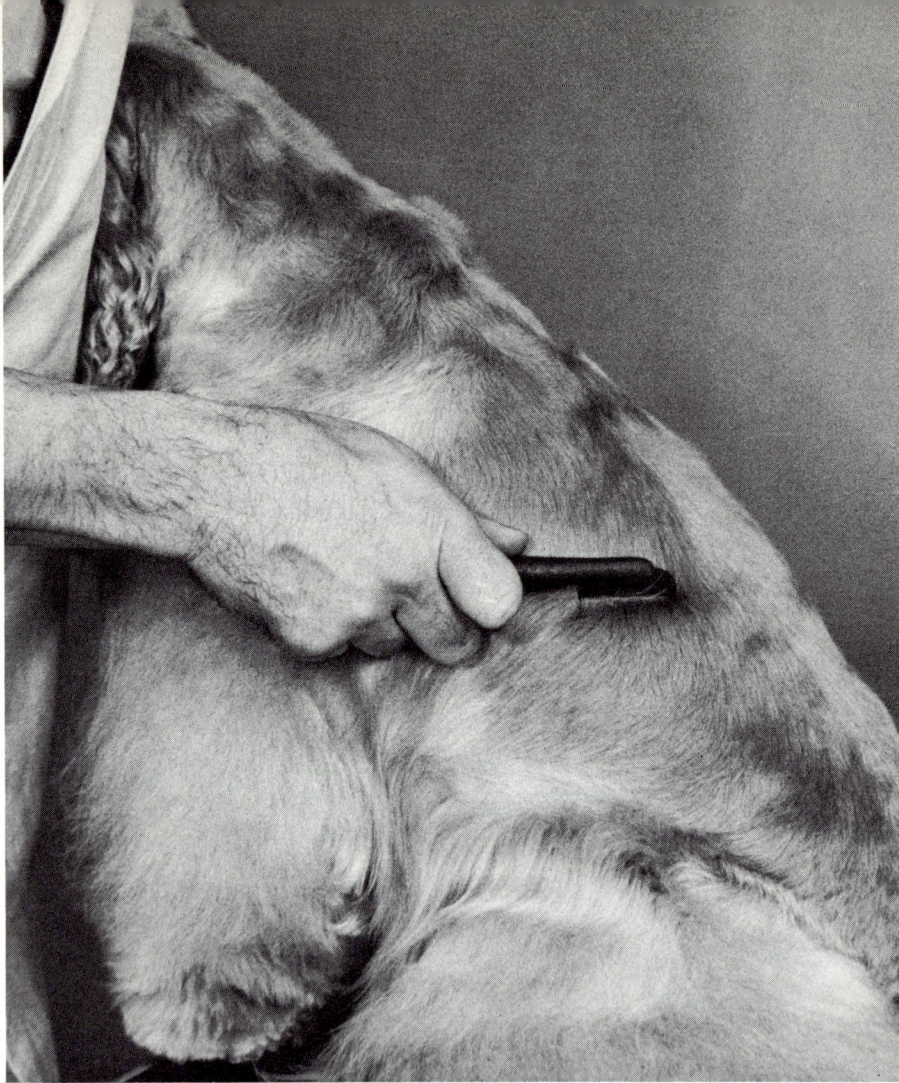

6-7. Carding

Carding

Certain types of coat, especially the buffs, may be very tight and require very little thinning. This type of coat may have a heavy, fuzzy undercoat showing through which can best be removed by "carding" (raking through the coat to remove the excess undercoat). Stand in front of the dog and lay the stripping knife flat on the coat with the teeth pointing away from you and tilted slightly downward (*Photo 6-7*); then gently push the blade through the coat with a long firm stroke, working with the grain and following the contour of the dog. Do this regularly over the entire body area, *but never over the feathering,* until the coat lays close and tight. A hacksaw blade is an ideal tool for carding a fine coat. The serrated blade of your thinning shears works very well for a dense coat.

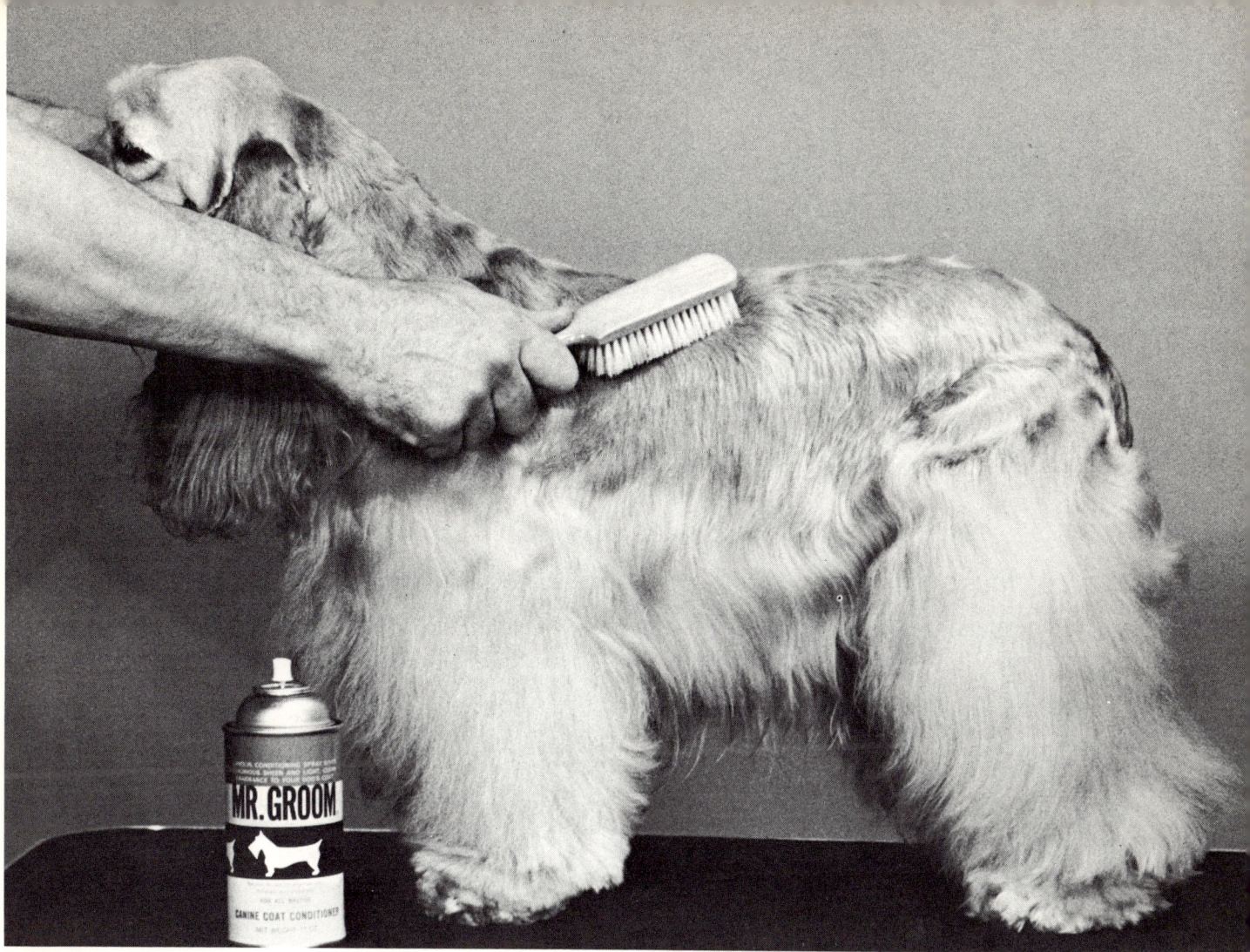

6-8.   Use of Bristle Brush

Maintaining the Coat

Acquiring a good coat on a Spaniel or a Setter requires both time and patience. It does not happen overnight, and cannot be achieved at all without regular attention. The period required to grow and build the coat will vary among breeds and among individual dogs. Some strains may take as long as three years before they coat up. Others are "foolers" and will coat up very quickly only to shed without warning. There are no hard and fast rules, and everyone must learn, by some degree of trial and error, how long it will take to bring any one particular dog to its peak of condition.

Grooming should be done in several stages over a period of about a month, depending on the breed. The head, ears, and throat are done first. Because the hair on these areas has to be kept short, clipping must be repeated as often

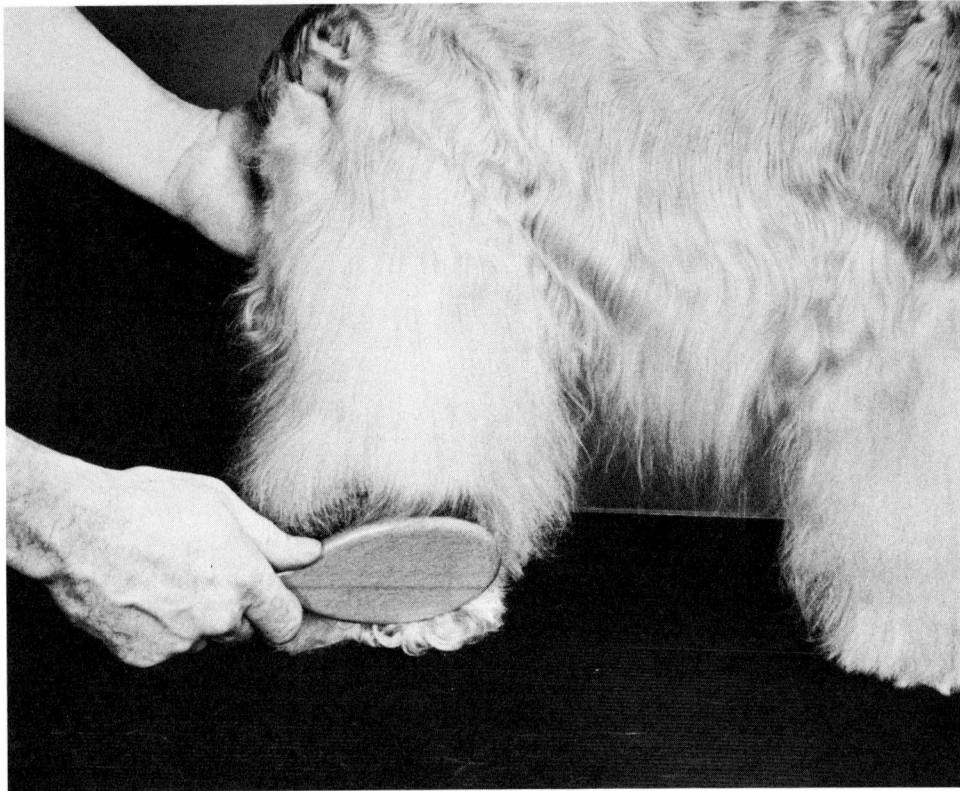

6-9. Pin Brush

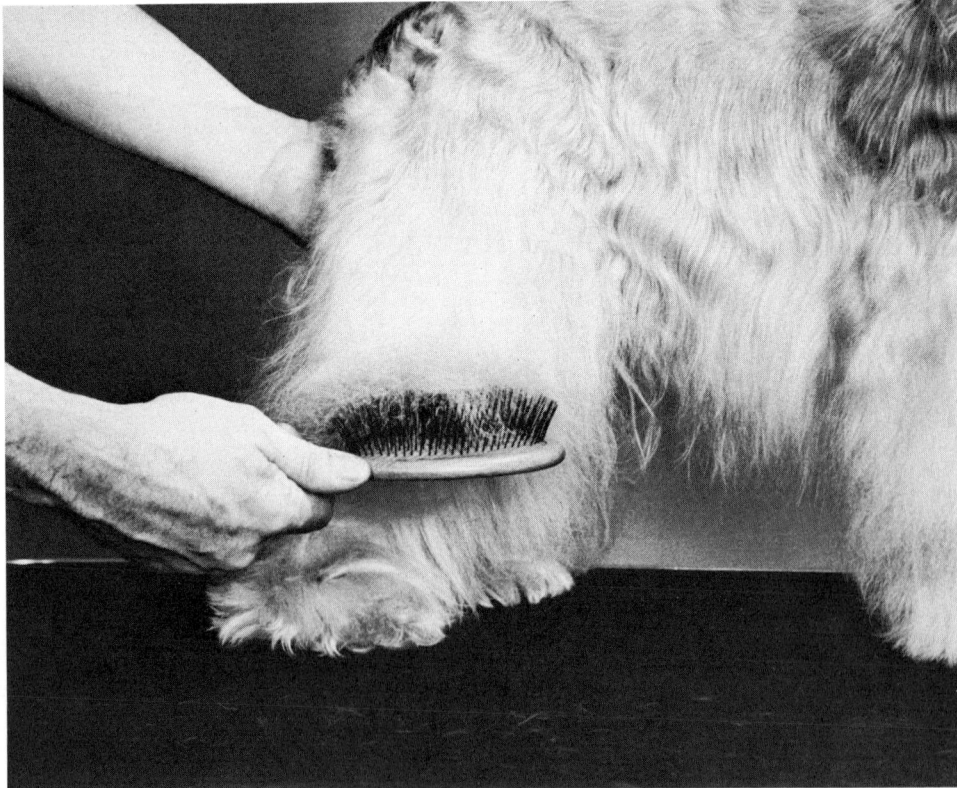

6-10. Pin Brush

as is required to maintain the desired appearance; approximately once a month on the average. This is followed by thinning the neck and shoulder, front, rear, and tail. Finally the body and feet.

After your dog has been completely groomed there is little to do for the next week or two, apart from keeping the feathering in shape, and brushing lightly with a natural bristle brush or hound glove two or three times a week. So concentrate on getting him into good physical condition as suggested elsewhere in this book.

Once the dog has been groomed for show, care becomes doubly important. After the routine preliminaries have been taken care of, spray a liberal amount of coat conditioner over the body and brush briskly for at least fifteen minutes using a hound glove or natural bristle brush (*Photo 6-8*). Special attention should be given to problem areas, such as the shoulders and hips. Most dogs enjoy this part of grooming and will brace contentedly against the pressure of the brush.

Weekly carding should also be introduced at about this time to prevent the undercoat from building up excessively.

Correct use of the pin brush not only serves to brush out the feathering and removes unwanted dead hair, but also stimulates additional growth to help produce the dense feathering that is so desirable, yet so difficult to acquire.

Holding the pin brush in the normal fashion, brush briskly from underneath, pressing the pins into the feathering. Rotate the pin brush lightly to massage the skin by making a half turn with your wrist. Do this several times in each area. When done correctly the hair will cling to the pins (*Photos 6-9 and 6-10*). Work over the feathering as shown. If you find that you are removing too much hair you should carefully review your technique. Should the feathering become very wispy and fly-away it may be necessary to tip the ends; this constitutes taking approximately half an inch off the length with the thinning shears about once a month until the feathering thickens up again.

PART III

The Other Sporting Breeds

CHAPTER 7

ENGLISH COCKER, ENGLISH SPRINGER, ENGLISH, IRISH, AND GORDON SETTERS

The grooming requirements for the above breeds are basically the same for pet or show, but are more in the nature of just "tidying up." The importance of a *natural* appearance cannot be over-stressed. The elegant look of these sporting dogs is lost when too much clipping is done.

Variation in the conformation of the different breeds automatically results in a dissimilar appearance of each breed. This can also apply among specimens of the same breed and must be expected. These facts are mentioned so as not to inhibit the novice groomer. While theory has its merits, only practice and experience with one or more breeds can develop knowledge and skill. Eventually we all develop a style of our own which becomes our trademark.

Ears, Head and Throat

Some knowledgeable groomers contend that the heads of the English Cocker and English Springer Spaniel are best clipped *against* the grain. We think that this is needlessly drastic, except on the ears, and that with limited exceptions the best effect is achieved by clipping *with* the grain using a No. 10 blade (*Diagram 8*).

There are occasions when better results can be obtained with a stripping knife or a razor comb. It is each groomer's responsibility to become familiar with such refinements once the basic steps have been mastered. By following the instructions contained in this book and studying the illustrations, many common errors can be avoided.

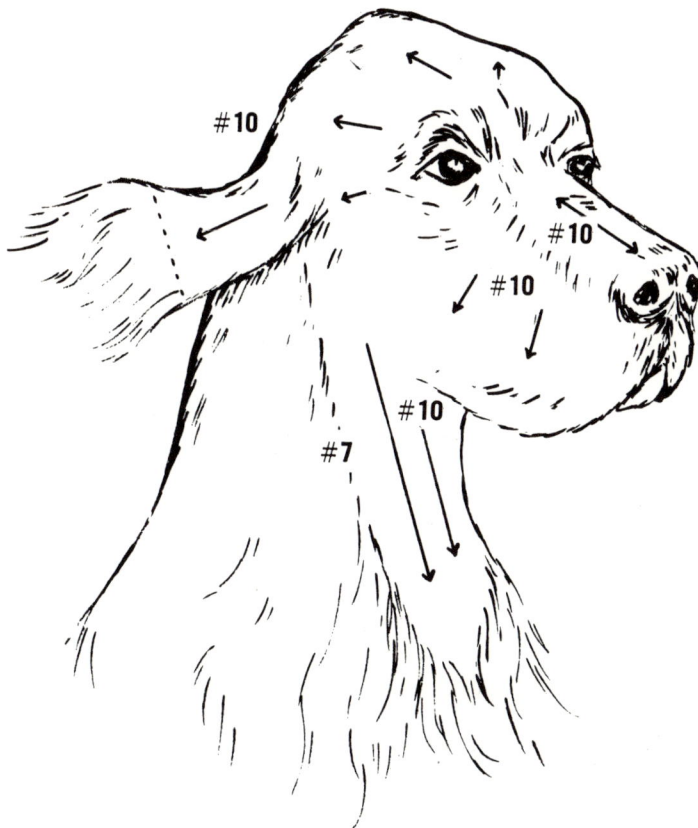

Diagram 8. Head Chart

The head may be clipped as described in the pet Cocker section of this book. However, there are three important differences that should be noted:

1. There should *not* be any long hair left above the brow; rather the reverse. The indentation between the supercillary arches must be thoroughly cleaned out.

2. The U at the throat should *not* extend to the sternum, but about midway to the sternum, approximately 4 to 6 inches in most cases.

3. A No. 10 of No. 7 blade can be used over the side of the neck, from below the ear, over the upper arm to the elbow. This is the procedure most frequently used for grooming the English Springer (*Diagram 9*).

The Body

The body coat may be treated in several ways:

1. It can be thinned with the thinning shears or stripping knife (show trim).

2. It can be carded to remove dead hair or woolly undercoat. (*See instructions*, "Grooming For Show").

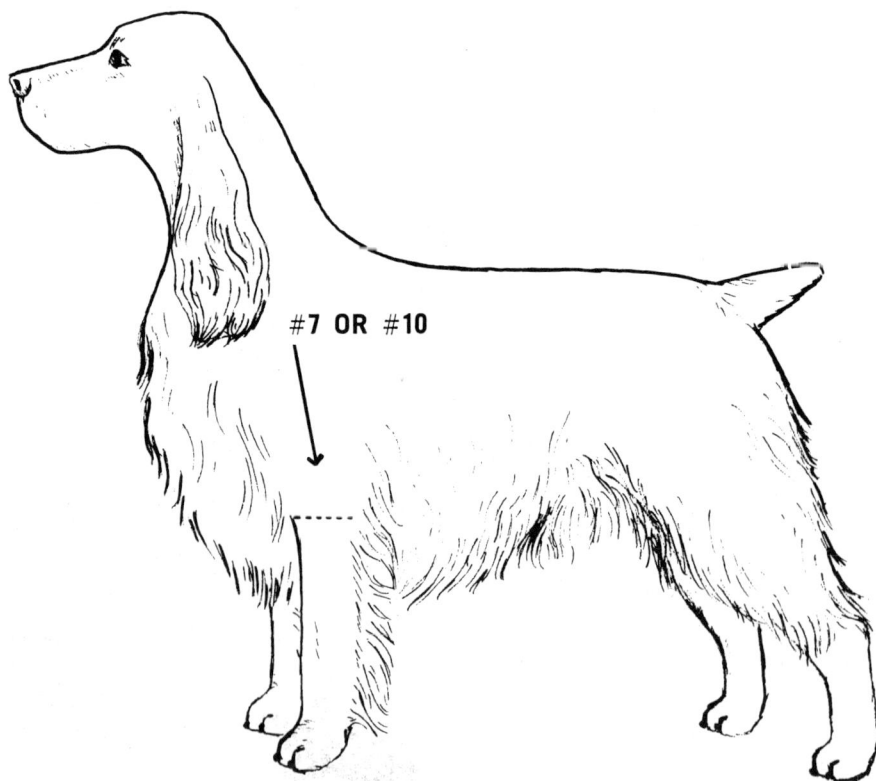

#7 OR #10

Diagram 9.   English Springer Spaniel

3. It can be thinned with the clippers.

4. A combination of the above three steps.

"Thinning" (3) is done by holding the clipper with a No. 7 blade at right angles to the dog's body and "combing" the coat lightly with the grain using overlapping strokes and following the contour of the body. This method is ideal for pet clips.

Whichever method you choose, the final step must be to blend in the various levels with the thinning shears.

Legs

Trim the back of the hocks free of long hair with the thinning shears on the three Setters and the English Springer (*Photo 7-1*). The English Cocker hocks are left natural (*see Diagram 10—Photo 7-2*). Trim straggly hair from the front part of the forelegs either with the thinning shears or a stripping knife. To save time, very bad cases can be clipped with a No. 7 blade before starting with the shears or stripper.

7-1. Trimming Hocks

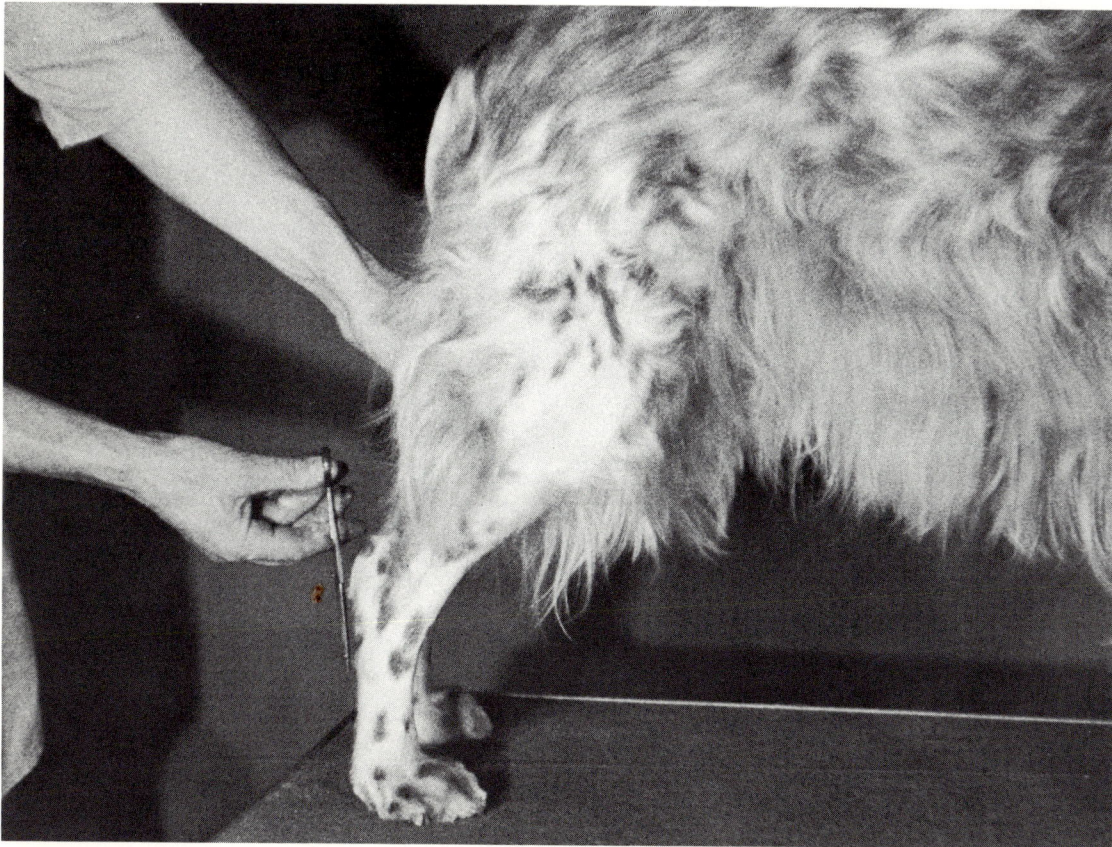

Diagram 10. English Cocker

7-2. English Cocker

Feet

The feet of all the sporting breeds in this section make an important contribution to the overall impression of the dog, and should always appear to be *tight and compact,* even if they are not!

Comb out any mats from in between the toes. Do not cut mats out with scissors, except as a last resort, because an unsightly gap will be left between the toes. Clip the hair in between the pads using a No. 10 blade. Next, clip the outer edges of the feet. This will make the foot look considerably smaller. Comb the hair up from in between the toes and scissor it level with the top of the foot. Scissor around the toes, including around the nails (*Photo 7-3*). Chalking, as described elsewhere in this book, will assist in filling the gaps in between the toes.

7-3.   Trimmed Foot (right)

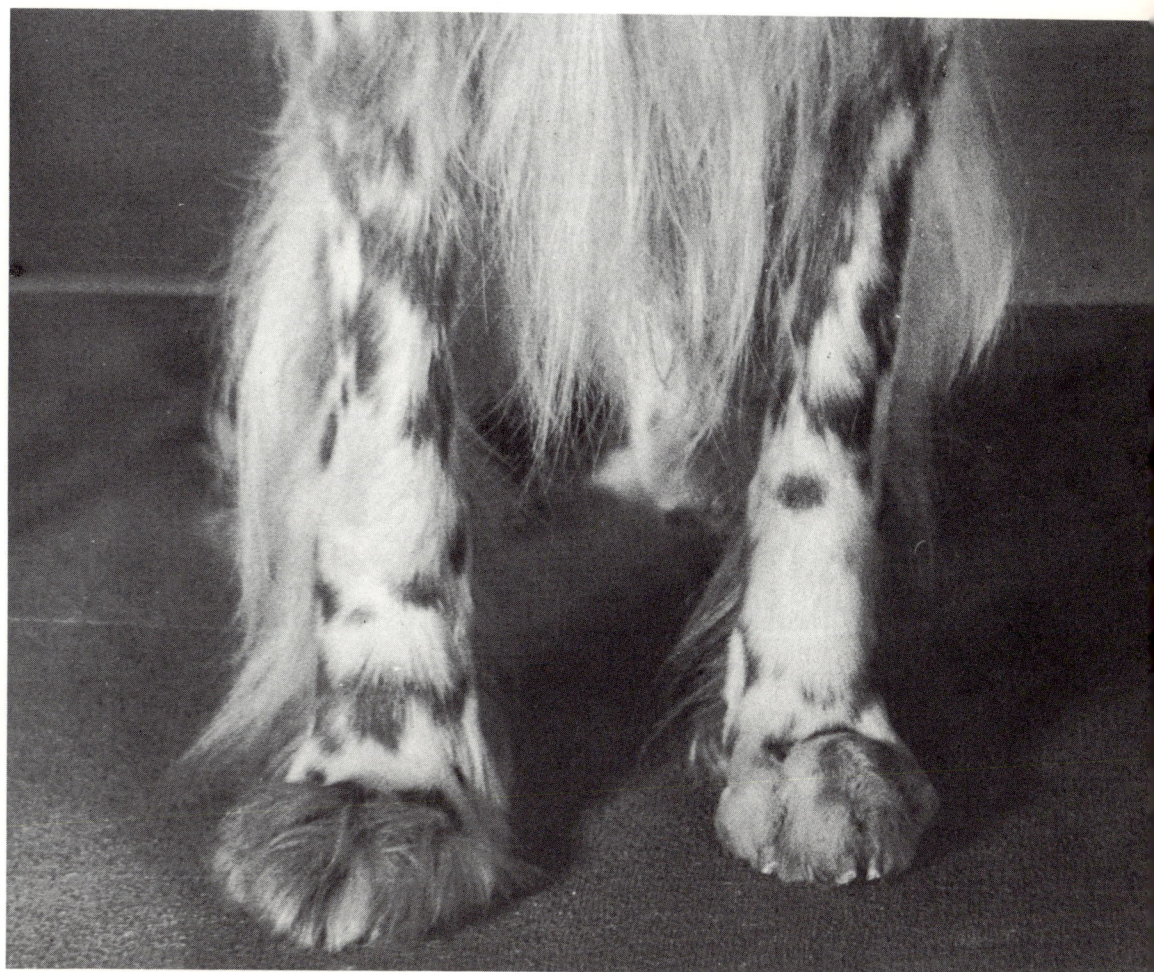

Before   After

Spaniel and Setter Tails

Spaniel tails may be trimmed as described in the section under American Cocker (*Diagram 11*). Setter tails require special attention. Trim about three inches of the underside of the tail with the thinning shears. Extend the tail horizontally, giving it a gentle shake, then with the shears shape to taper gently to a point at the tip (*Diagram 12*). Remove surplus hair from the top of the tail with thinning shears or stripping knife. When you are finished study *Diagram 12* for overall effect.

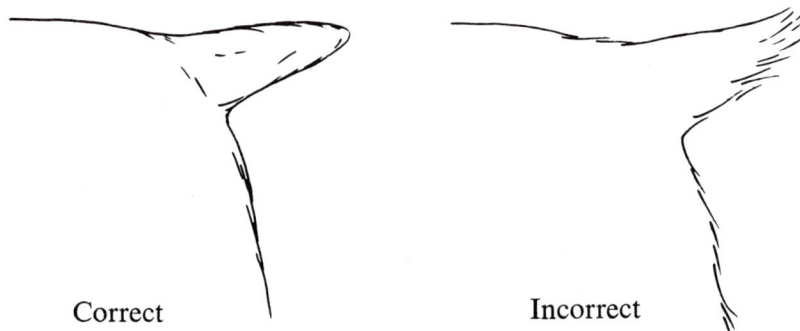

Correct

Incorrect

Diagram 11.   Spaniel Tails

Diagram 12.   Setter

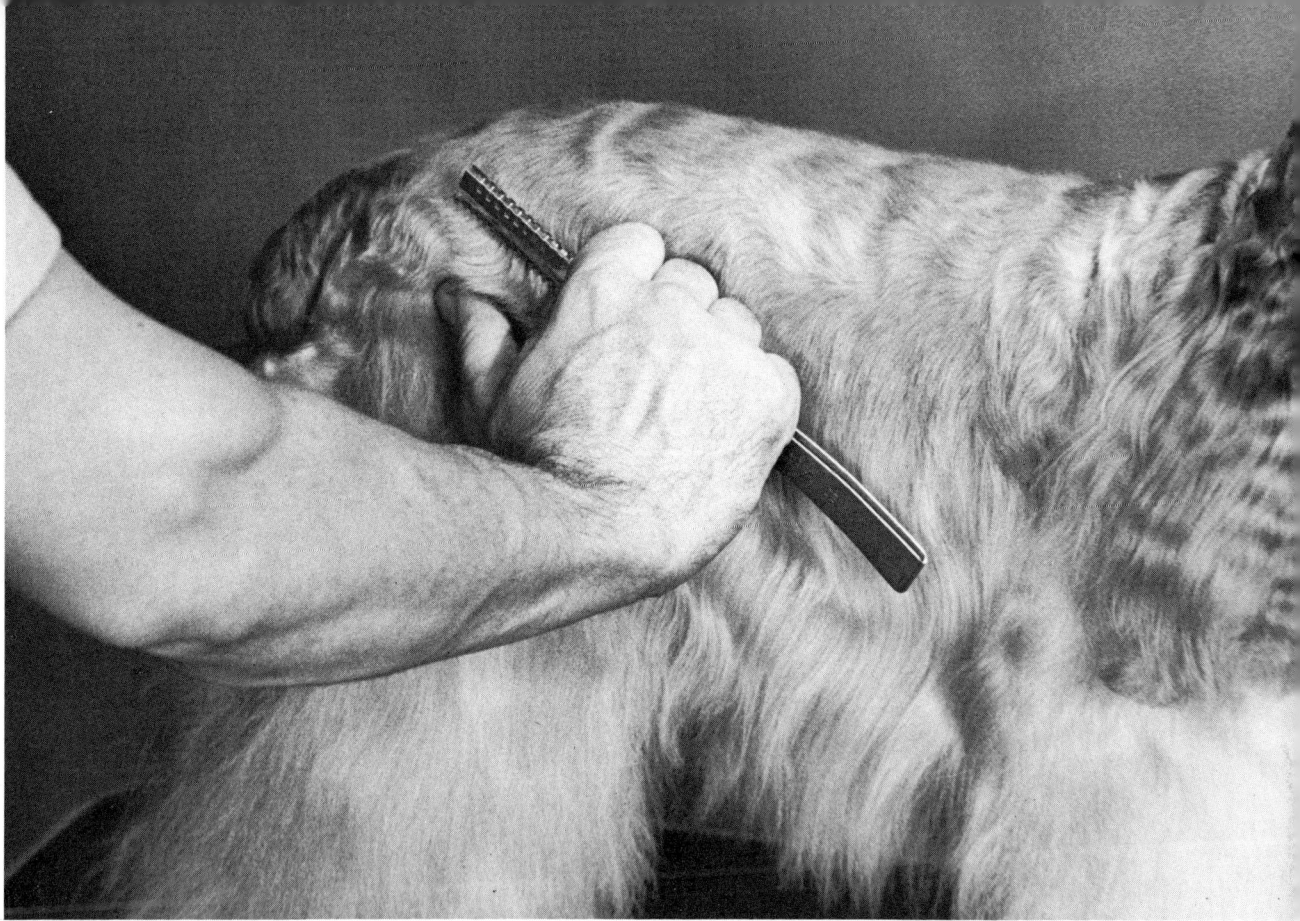

7-4. Thinning the Coat (using a razor comb)

The Stripping Knife and Razor Comb

Unlike the technique used for stripping Terrier breeds, the stripping knife is used to *cut* the coat instead of being used merely to hold the coat to facilitate plucking it out. Hold the stripping knife as if you were thumbing through the pages of a book and ruff a small amount of coat with your thumb. Leaving your thumb under the displaced hair, bring the blade of the stripping knife into contact with your thumb by gently clenching your hand, trapping the hair between the blade and your thumb (*Photo 7-4*), and with a rolling wrist motion similar to the action used to core an apple, cut the coat. As you perform this action, allow part of the hair to slip through under your thumb. This will have the effect of graduating the coat. Work over the area with slightly overlapping strokes until you achieve the desired effect. There is no reason why a razor comb should not be used where the coat is heavy.

The above method is especially suitable for grooming the English Cocker and English Setter (*Diagram 12—Photo 7-5*).

Field Clip

Sportsmen frequently want their dogs groomed for hunting; this type of clip is often referred to as a "Field Clip." It consists of the same basic procedures previously described except that in the Field Clip the furnishings are trimmed short with either the thinning shears or No. 7 blade. The purpose of grooming the dog in this fashion is to prevent the coat from becoming tangled in heavy cover, and also to make the the removal of burrs from the coat an easier task. The body coat should not be taken down too short because this will rob the dog of its protection against the sharp pointed briars. No clipping should be done against the grain for this same reason. The Field Clip is the same for all breeds where the utilitarian value is more important than an elegant appearance.

7-5.   English Setter

7-6. Irish Setter

7-7. Gordon Setter

CHAPTER 8

FINE POINTS

It is essential to master the fine points of the art of dog grooming. Learning the basic skills is not enough for the sporting-dog groomer who wants to do a professional-looking job. Did you neglect to pluck the ears or trim the nails? Is the dog completely clean? Have you avoided all clipper burns and rashes?

Very often these extra little attentions distinguish the good groomer from the mediocre one. If the groomer is a professional, his knowledge of these small but important matters will help cement the relationship between his customers and himself. Many dog owners will travel far out of their way to patronize a favorite groomer. What a happy advertisement it is for the professional when a patron's dog arrives happily wagging his tail!

Ear Plucking

Purchase a can of ear powder (*Photo 8-1*) from your pet dealer before you begin to clean your dog's ears. Shake a little of it into the ear and spread it through the hairs. This will cause the hairs to become dry and brittle so that

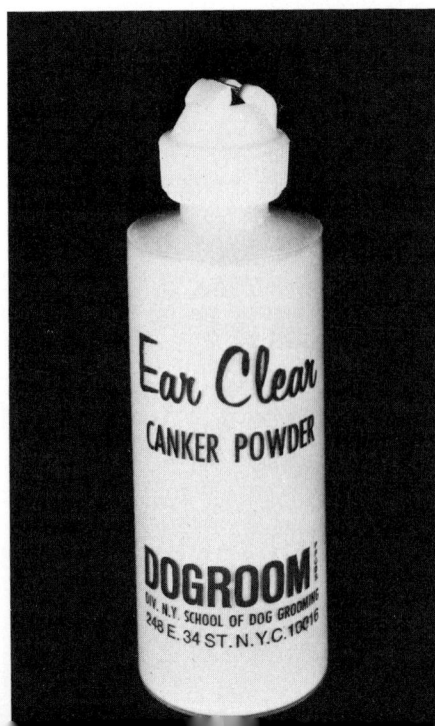

8-1. Ear Powder

they are easier to pull out. In the beginning use your fingers to pluck out the hair; later, when you are more experienced, use a pair of hemostats or ear pluckers (*Photo 8-2*). Pluck the hairs with a quick rolling motion; the entire job should take only a few moments.

The best time to clean the dog's ears is before his bath, at the same time that you trim his nails, so that any trace of liquid or powder left on the coat will be washed away.

Never attempt to treat the dog's ears if they are infected. This is a matter for the veterinarian.

Nail Trimming

City dogs are generally house pets, and in the high-storied apartments where they make their homes they seldom get enough exercise. Consequently, their nails do not receive the natural grinding which comes with a reasonable amount of outdoor activity, and they have to be trimmed regularly.

8-2. Ear Plucking

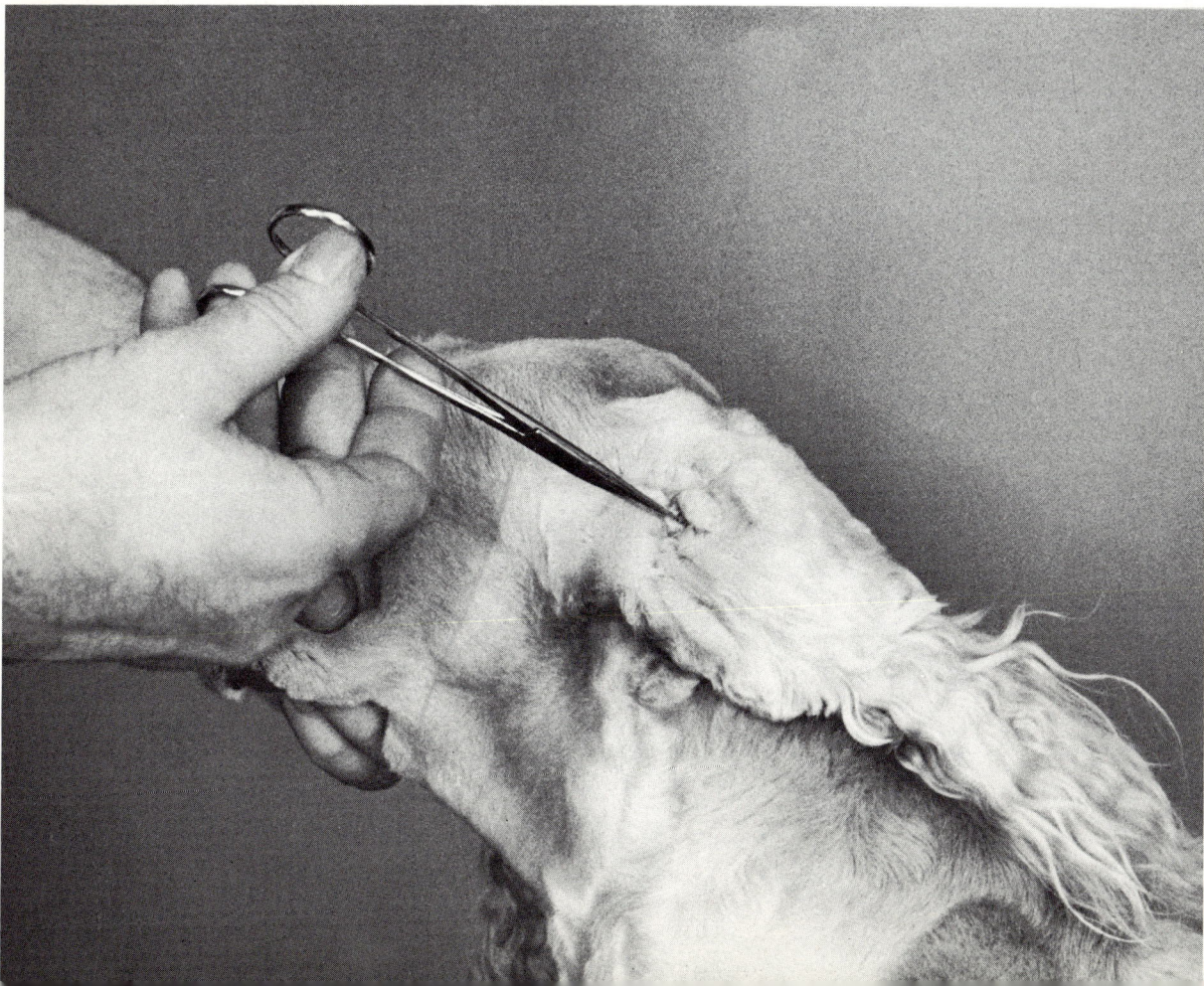

The thing to be concerned about here is the "quick" under the nail. The novice should be content to trim just the tips at first. This is done by holding the paw firmly and trimming with short, decisive strokes (*Photo 8-3*). Be sure to check the dog for dewclaws (the inside nails on the front paws which should normally be removed by the vet when the puppy is a few days old). If dewclaws are present and not trimmed, they will eventually curl and hamper the dog's walking.

When you become familiar with this nail trimming operation, you will know exactly how high up on the nail you can go without causing bleeding. But until you do, it is wise to play it safe. If bleeding should occur, have a can of "Cut Stop" (*Photo 8-4*) or Monsell Solution on hand which will stop the flow of blood immediately. These medications are available at most pet shops or drugstores in both powder and liquid form.

The best time to trim the dog's nails is just before his bath. The worst time, as many groomers have discovered to their sorrow, is at the end of the grooming job when the dog is beautifully turned out. If the nails are trimmed at this point and bleeding occurs, the coat may become smeared and the job ruined.

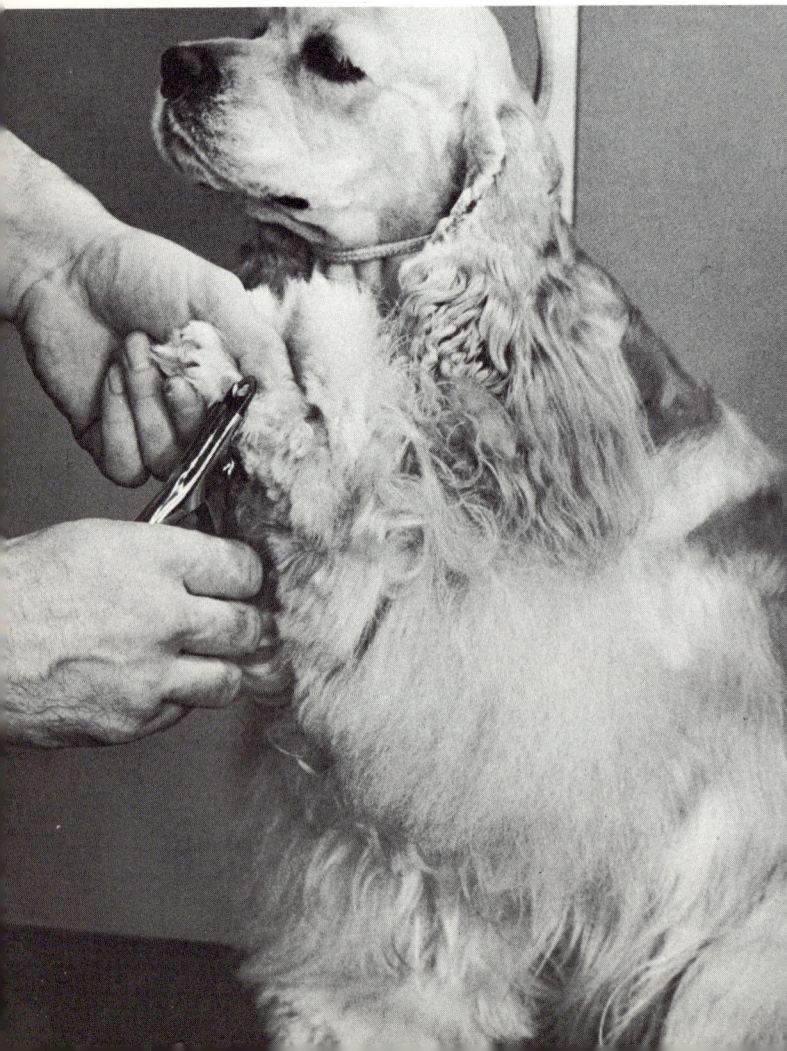

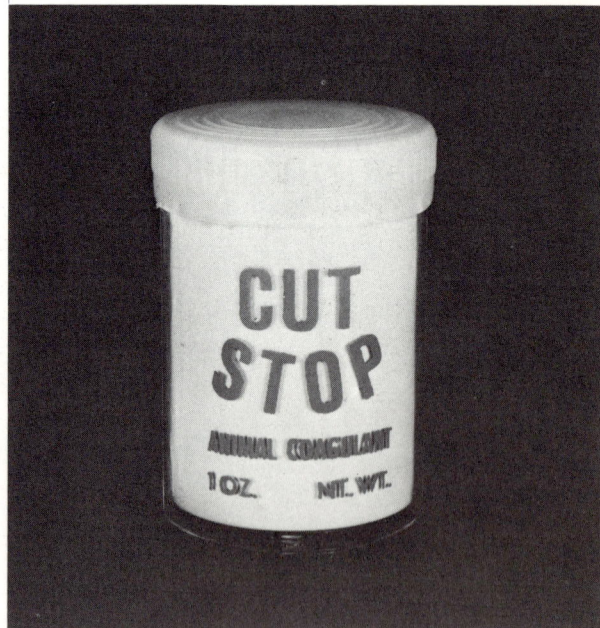

8-4. Cut Stop

8-3. Nail Trimming

Chalking

In the case of light or predominantly white dogs the problem of maintaining that sparkling, clean appearance is solved by using white chalk as a cleaning agent. White chalk also makes the feathering thicker and easier to control. In doggie parlance, "chalking" refers to the practice of brushing *any* substance into the coat. In the sporting breeds, corn starch and baby powder are used as much as anything else.

Chalk comes in either powdered form or in a block, and may be applied when the coat is wet or dry. The general practice is to use powdered chalk or corn starch on the wet coat and block chalk or talc for dry applications or touch-up work. If the dog is being exhibited, all traces of powder must be removed from the coat before the dog enters the ring, as specified in *AKC Show Regulations*.

For wet application the feathering should be sponged down, using a minimum amount of tepid water, and then dried with a towel. The white areas of the body should be sponged on the surface sufficiently to dampen the coat.

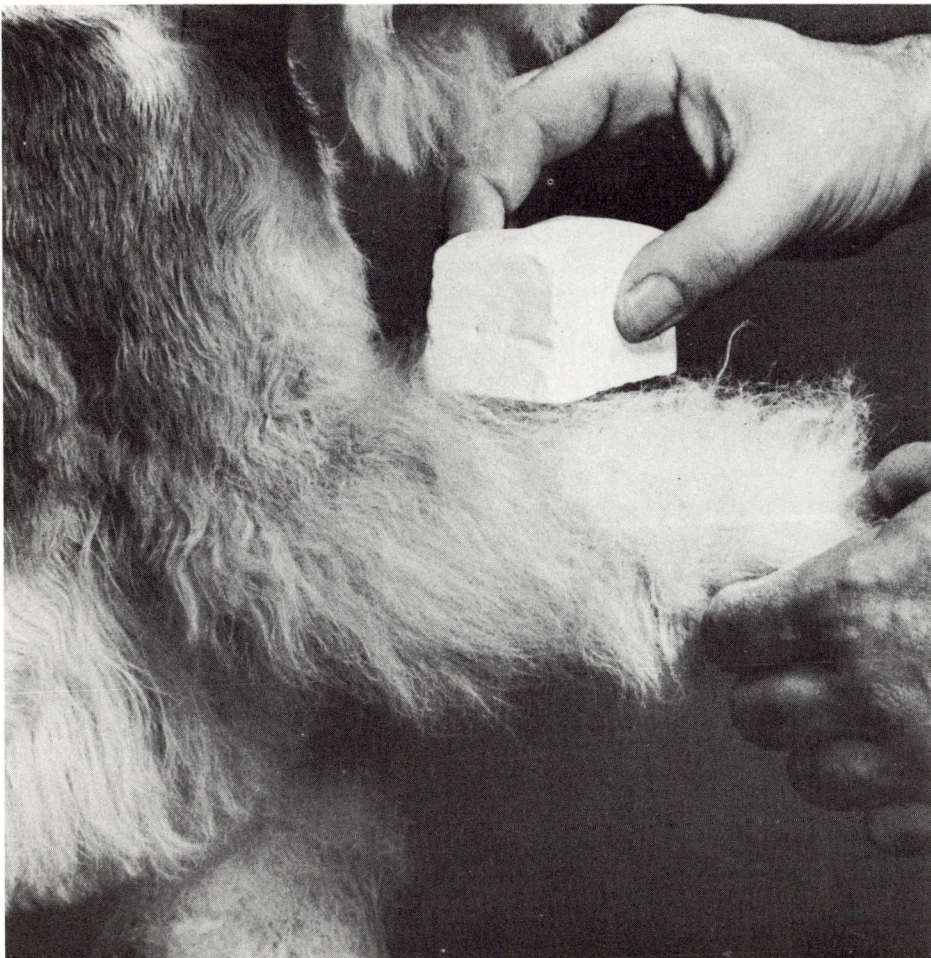

8-5. Block Chalk

65

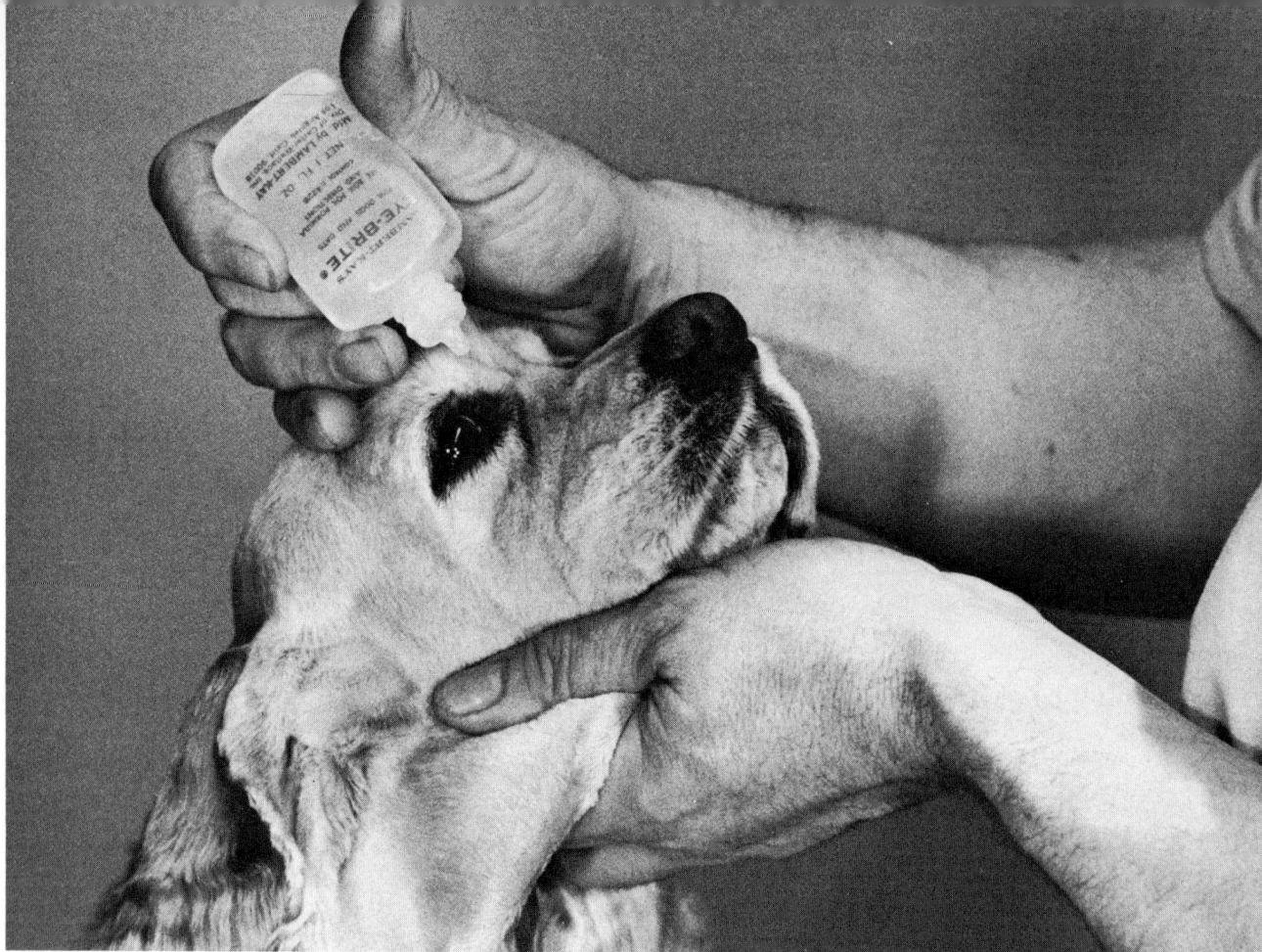

8-6. Eye Drops

Apply a dusting of chalk to the feet, including in between the toes to make the feet appear more compact; to the leg furnishing (*Photo 8-5*), if the feathering is predominently white, and also to the underchest. Use a bristle brush, working the powder into the hair with a light inward motion. On the body areas the chalk should be applied with the grain of the hair and special care should be taken to avoid overpowdering colored areas, as in the case of particolors. The area above the eyes can be chalked without undue fuss by taking a pinch of chalk between the fingers and applying it carefully while the dog's head is inclined downward. After chalking, the dog can be *sacked up* if desired, to help flatten the coat, and then placed in a warm confined area until completely dry after which all surplus powder must be brushed out. Again a pure bristle brush is best for this purpose. A note on the eyes: during chalking, dust can easily get into the dog's eyes. Apply eye drops (*Photo 8-6*) to remove irritating particles and to soothe the eyes after chalking and brushing has been completed.

66

CHAPTER 9

MISCELLANEOUS

Grooming and taking care of dogs is not for lazy people, but neither is the work unpleasant or overly difficult. Many dog owners become professionals simply because they are so fond of their own animals. Several of these men and women now hold top positions in the dog world.

Whether done by a professional or amateur, expert or beginner, the grooming process should be a pleasure—not an ordeal—for both dog and groomer. The ideal relationship is one where the dog looks forward to being groomed. The whole process is much easier when the dog is not frightened or nervous.

Clipper Burns and Rashes

Occasionally pet owners say that their dogs come back from grooming salons with clipper burns and rashes. These owners often claim that the dog did not have anything like that before going to the grooming shop and that their veterinarians diagnosed clipper burn. Occasionally this may be true—there are, of course, times when the grooming salon is at fault. As a rule, however, this will not happen at a reputable grooming salon. Dogs, like people, vary in skin sensitivity. Some have very tender skins and show such marks after a close clipping. When a clipper burn does develop in spite of the best precautions, you can apply any one of a half dozen soothing lotions specially prepared for dogs. In addition, try not to clip the sensitive spots as close the next time.

Clipper burns may also develop if the clippers are allowed to run so long that the blades get too hot. To avoid this the groomer must cool (or change) the blade occasionally during the clipping. A hot blade can be instantly cooled, lubricated, and sanitized with "Oster" Clipper Spray. Before this product came on the market, the process took much longer. It was necessary to change the blades frequently or to stop and wait until the blade cooled down.

Clipping the dog before his bath is another cause of clipper rash. As the reader will recall, at the beginning of this book, the necessity of thoroughly brushing and bathing the dog before clipping was well stressed. The alternative can lead to discomfort and, perhaps, infection from the combination of hot clippers and dirty skin. Also it is much easier to clip a clean dog.

If, despite all precautions, the dog's skin still becomes irritated, have him checked by a veterinarian.

Fleas

Fleas are not only a discomfort to your dog but also a major cause of potentially dangerous worm infections. Don't waste any time in combating fleas once they appear. There are several goood insecticide shampoos on the market that are easy to apply. So, use a flea shampoo instead of a regular shampoo.

Ticks

There are several hundred species of ticks, although only two, the Brown Dog Tick, and the American Dog Tick, (a variety of wood tick) are of importance to the dog. There is a danger of infestation, and the matter cannot be treated lightly. To remove one or a few ticks, clamp a pair of Kelly forceps onto the tick as close to the dog's skin as possible over the site where the head is buried. Wait for a few moments and withdraw the tick—making certain that you also got the tick's head—and dispose of it. In the event of a bad infestation, the dog should be dipped in a special solution manufactured for this purpose. If you are going to treat the badly infested dog yourself, a good tick dip is available in any pet shop. However, it is better to let a veterinarian do the job.

If you find ticks on your dog, make certain to check for ticks around the dog's sleeping area and all other areas where the dog usually rests.

Ticks can carry many diseases that are deadly to humans—especially to young children—so never neglect to check all around your home if you suspect the presence of ticks.

Worms

The health of your dog is an important part of his preshow preparation. A well-conditioned dog will always look the part, and a dull, listless specimen will not impress regardless of how carefully groomed he may be. Conditioning must start from the inside, and the first step is to insure that your dog is

68

free of internal parasites. This is another job for your vet. Many dog owners do not realize that the most debilitating types of worms are not readily visible to the naked eye and that a microscopic examination of the dog's stool is the only reliable method of determining the presence of worms.

Teeth Cleaning

The need to scale a dog's teeth occurs more frequently today than it used to. One of the reasons is the modern method of feeding.

The manufacturers of Milk Bones (dog biscuits) claim that their product will remove tartar if given regularly over a period of three weeks.

Many old-time groomers used the edge of a coin, such as a nickel or dime to crack the tartar accumulation on the teeth, and that method still works well. The professional method is to use a rongeur forceps to crack the tartar (*Photo 9-1*). A scraper is then used to remove any minute amounts that remain attached (*Photo 9-2*). Following this, the teeth can be polished by using a small amount of kitchen cleanser on a piece of damp cotton swab. If the dog's gums are inflamed or the teeth loosen or have cavities and require extraction, the person best qualified to deal with the problem is the veterinarian.

9-1. Rongeur Forceps

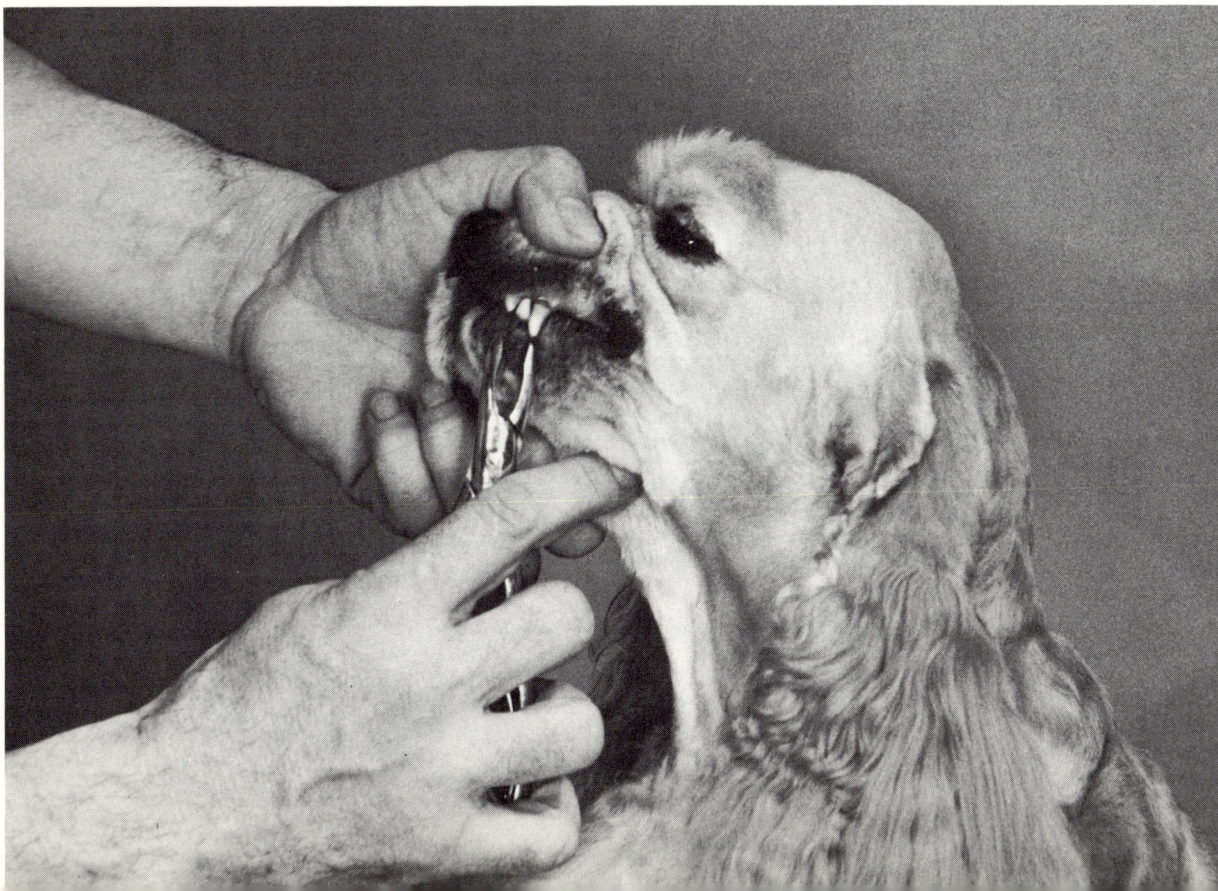

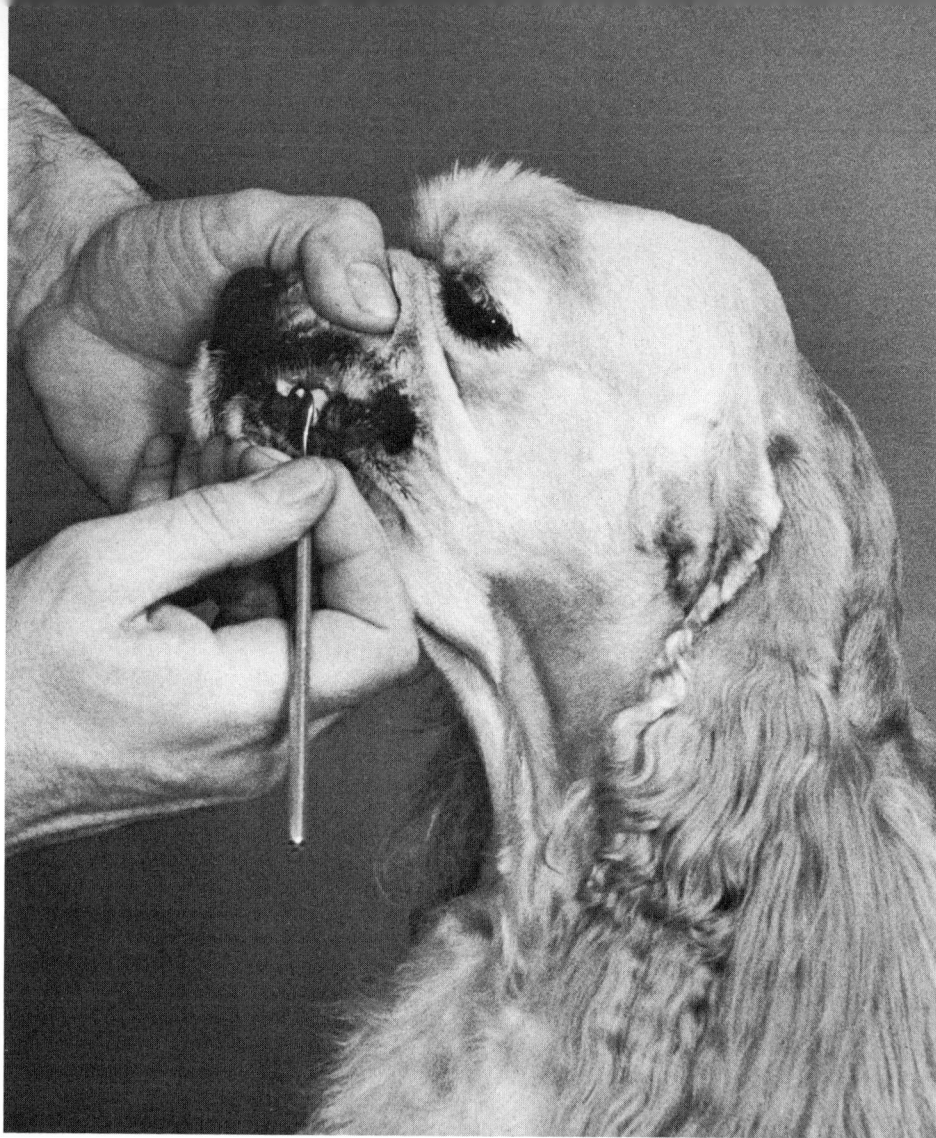

9-2. Tooth Scraper

Anal Glands

The anal sacs are located between the internal and external sphincter muscles, on either side of the lower portion of the anus. The specific function of the organ remains undetermined, but a recent theory suggests that it may serve as a means of protection for the weaker and older animals. In moments of extreme fear, involuntary elimination of the anal sacs occurs resulting in a pungent odor unpleasant to humans. Incorrect expressing of the anal sacs could cause an abscess, but there are occasions when they become impacted, creating discomfort to the dog, and must be treated. This procedure is rather distasteful to the average person and again, is best left to your veterinarian.

70

Feeding and Exercise

"We are what we eat." Whoever made that observation had the right idea, and dogs, as well as people, need a well balanced diet. The best thing to feed your dog is food designed for him—not a human diet. People who, in a misguided act of kindness, add table scraps to their dog's food to make it more palatable, may find that their dogs will eventually become very "picky" and, consequently, get into poor condition.

There are many theories of what is the best diet for dogs, and even the experts disagree on this subject. Find a veterinarian that has been recommended to you and ask him for advice on what to feed your dog. Or you may wish to ask a breeder whose dogs you especially admire.

Dry, flaky skin or a dull coat, excessive shedding, itching, and scratching without evidence of parasites, may be a symptom of fatty acid deficiency. A few drops of Lambert-Kay's "Linatone" added to a balanced diet may help to curb this condition and enhance the beauty and luster of the coat.

Controlled exercise in the form of daily road work undoubtedly is the best form of conditioning for any breed of dog. Walking will rapidly improve muscle tone, tighten up the feet, and grind down the nails. If possible, walk your dog several miles every day. That you, too, will look and feel fitter, may be a little extra bonus. Why not extend the benefits of jogging to include your dog?

What Is a Show Dog?

Being American Kennel Club registered is only part of the requirement for a show dog. The dog must also qualify as a representative of its breed by conforming to the AKC standard set up for that breed. Included in the standard are specifications which, if not complied with, incur mandatory disqualification from AKC competition. You may write to the American Kennel Club, 51 Madison Avenue, New York, New York 10016, for a copy of the standard for any recognized breed.

All dog show entries must be recorded on official entry forms. These may be obtained by writing to the superintendents of a particular show. A list of show superintendents is included in every issue of *Pure-Bred Dogs American Kennel Club Gazette,* a monthly magazine published by the AKC. The entry forms are self-explanatory.

Buying a Puppy

If you are interested in buying a puppy, go to a reputable breeder—that is, a person who has established a reputation for breeding and selling quality dogs. It will be cheaper in the long run, even if the puppy initially costs more than it would from some lesser known breeder. This is especially true if you are looking for a dog with show quality. In addition, it is important that the dog come from the type of breeder who will accustom him to being groomed and handled as soon as he is old enough. This will greatly reduce the chores of the new puppy owner who decides to do the grooming himself.

How often have we heard the lament, "We were promised papers, but we never got them." Make sure you either get the AKC registration forms from the breeder as soon as you buy the puppy or else suggest withholding a fraction of the payment until such time as the papers are made over to you. After all, if you buy an AKC registered puppy and never receive the registration papers, you have actually been given only a part of your purchase.

Have your puppy checked by a veterinarian immediately and make sure that the dog has had all his shots before you expose him to the outside world. The vet is your pet's doctor—always consult him if you are concerned about your puppy's health.

THE DOG GROOMING SALON

If you wish to go beyond trimming your own dog and turn your hobby into a profitable career, proper schooling, while not yet required by law in many states, is, of course, necessary. Obviously, this book cannot substitute for a complete professional course which lasts many weeks. If you decide to turn professional, attend a licensed school and take an advanced course such as the one given by the New York School of Dog Grooming. In the long run, it will be the most worthwhile part of your investment (as well as the cheapest).

Dog grooming salons are flourishing all over the country, and in the past few years, they have become an industry in themselves. Indeed, pets—breeding them, caring for them, and grooming them—have become big business.

While the Poodles and Terriers are indisputably the leading breeds in the country and largely responsible for the healthy condition of the dog grooming business, the combined Spaniel and Setter breeds do not run far behind. Moreover, the fact that the pet Spaniel and Setters can be clipped in half the time that it takes to clip the Poodle makes them far more profitable to deal with. Indeed, there is a certain trend, especially in the larger cities, toward dog grooming shops that specialize in breeds other than poodles.

A dog grooming career is attractive to many people because it permits them to combine both avocation and vocation and to establish a profitable business out of something they like to do. Dog grooming is a growing and profitable field, and the initial investment is relatively low.

10-1. Cages and Cage Dryers

A major part of the investment will go into equipment. A professional groomer requires professional tools. The following equipment is absolutely essential:

Cages, preferably of galvanized metal or steel (*Photo 10-1*).

Cage dryer for drying.

Bathtub—can be a regular model but must stand or be elevated to a waist-high position (*Photo 10-2*).

Floor dryer for fluffing.

Grooming table with post and loop.

Clippers, blades, shampoos, brushes, combs, nail trimmers, scissors, ear powders, ear plucker, etc. (*Photo 10-3*), as well as all the necessary cleaning equipment.

A good vacuum cleaner—we recommend an "Industrial Shop Vacuum," which can be purchased at major department stores.

There are many more things to know about setting up a dog grooming salon. Naturally, it is beyond the scope of this book to go into details of this operation.

10-2. Bathtub, Waist-High

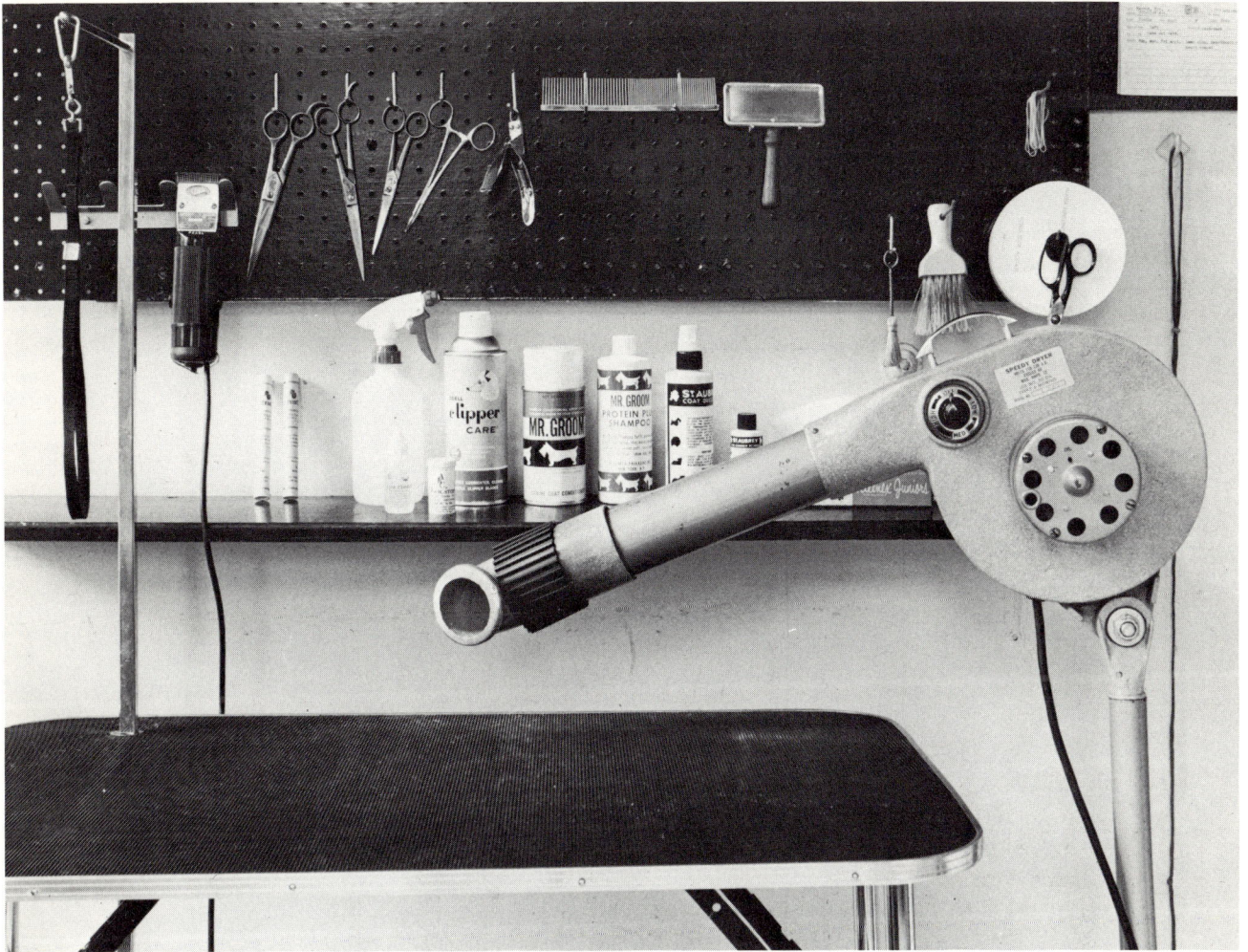

10-3. Professional Work Area

10-4. Interior of Canine Castle

CHAPTER 10

CONCLUSION

Regardless of whether you are interested in learning to groom your own pet or in making this your career, your primary goal should be to do the best possible job of grooming the dog.

Our advice to those who feel unsure about their ability to handle dogs is, "Take your time!" Before you invest in a shop of your own, go to a licensed school and get the necessary instruction. If you want to be a professional, learn how to groom all breeds.

Read as much theory as you can and acquaint yourself with the different breeds and their histories. Whether you are an individual Cocker or Setter owner or a professional groomer, the more you know about these dogs, the better off you'll be. It's amazing how many questions you'll be asked about your own dog or dogs in general.

How do you tell a good puppy from a poor one? What color is the best? How often should a bitch be mated? Where do we find a good stud? The answers to these questions and many more can be found in any comprehensive book on dogs.

Never attempt to act as a substitute veterinarian. A badly infected ear, a peculiar body growth, impacted anal glands, or any of the hundreds of other problems to which the dog is heir can be treated properly only by the man who has been trained to treat them.

Your own dog, too, can be a walking advertisement for you. An improperly cared for, uncomfortable-looking, unkempt, or over-pampered dog will never win you any friends or customers. On the other hand, an elegant beauty, striding gracefully alongside his master, is the most eloquent testimonial to you as the owner, handler, and groomer.

GLOSSARY OF TERMS

APRON—Long hair on chest.

BLOOM—Coat in ideal condition.

FEATHERING—Long fringe hair on ears, legs, tail, or body.

FLAG—Fringed tail.

SUPERCILIARY ARCHES—The brow.

SACKING OR WRAPPING—Pinning the dog into a large towel in order to flatten the coat.

CARDING—Combing or raking through the coat with a stripping knife to remove excess undercoat.

CONFORMATION—The physical structure of a dog corresponding to the official AKC Standard for that breed.

AKC—The American Kennel Club.

SHOW DOG—A dog that is eligible to compete for the title of "Champion" and is being exhibited at AKC shows for that purpose.

BREED STANDARD—The official specifications for each breed as drawn up by the parent breed club and approved by the AKC.

DISQUALIFICATION—A fault or demerit considered so detrimental to the welfare of the breed that any dog having such a fault is not allowed to compete at AKC shows, e.g., an American Cocker male over $15\frac{1}{2}$ inches at the shoulder or a female over $14\frac{1}{2}$ inches.

PURE BRED DOG—A dog whose parents are both of the same breed and who produce offspring consistent with the recognized standard for that breed.

LIST OF CREDITS

Breed	Name	Owner
American Cocker	Ch. Burson's Barney	Ruth M. Kraeuchi, St. Louis, Missouri
English Springer	Ch. Sal Lyn's Makers Mark	Mrs. Margaret Migliorini, Wyoming, Delaware
English Cocker	Ch. Kenobo Blue Astro	Helja Tushin and Bonnie Prockter
English Setter	Ch. Guys N Dolls Shalimar /Duke	Neal and Harron Weinstein, Chatworth, California
Gordon Setter	Ch. Hickory Harvest	Hickory Smoke Kennels
Irish Setter	Ch. Tirrelda Oberon Bruce	Hilton Cooper, Tallahassee, Florida